LION BRAND YARN

JUST**HATS**

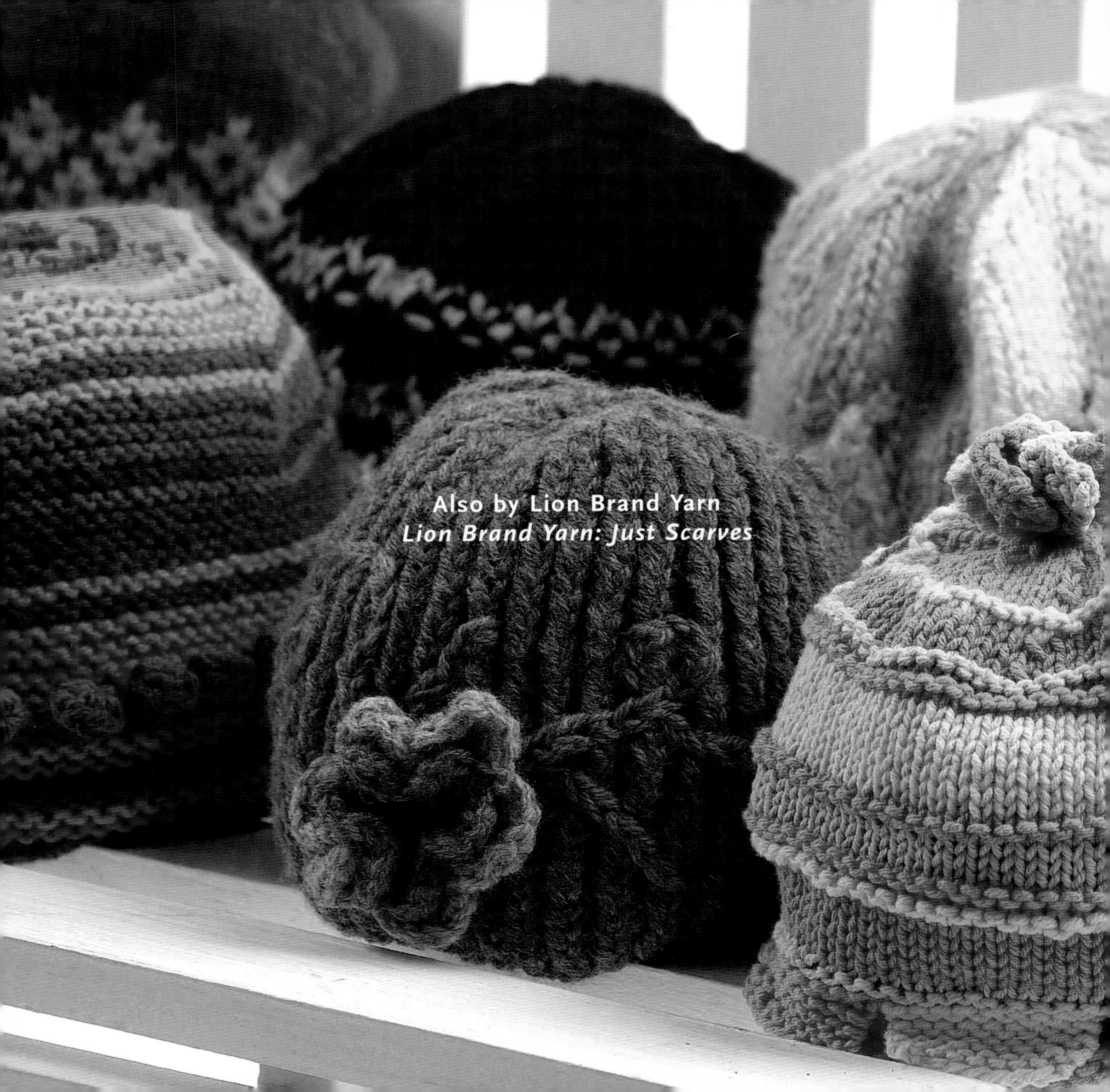

Also by Lion Brand Yarn

Lion Brand Yarn: Just Scarves

LION BRAND YARN

JUST**HATS**

FAVORITE PATTERNS TO KNIT AND CROCHET

EDITED BY NANCY J. THOMAS AND ADINA KLEIN

POTTER
CRAFT

NEW YORK

Acknowledgments
Editors: Nancy J. Thomas and Adina Klein
Associate Design Editor: Stephanie Klose
Photography: Jack Deutsch

The authors and publisher would like to thank the
Craft Yarn Council of America for providing the
yarn weight standards and accompanying icons
used in this book. For more information, please
visit www.YarnStandards.com.

Published in the United States by Potter Craft, an
imprint of the Crown Publishing Group, a division
of Random House, Inc., New York.

POTTER CRAFT and CLARKSON N. POTTER are
trademarks and POTTER and colophon are
registered trademarks of Random House, Inc.

Library of Congress Cataloging-in-Publication
Lion Brand. Just hats / edited by Nancy J. Thomas.
    1. Knitting—Patterns. 2. Crocheting—Patterns.
3. Hats. I. Title: Just hats. II. Thomas, Nancy J.
TT825.L5843   2005
746.43'20432—dc22   2004020109

ISBN: 1-4000-8059-2

Printed in Singapore

Design by Caitlin Daniels Israel

10   9   8   7   6   5   4   3   2

First Edition

CONTENTS

INTRODUCTION

Functional or fashionable, traditional or trendy, hats are great accessories to make and wear. From fast and easy toppers to projects using advanced techniques, hats are a sure route to knitting pleasure. They keep you warm in winter, protect you from the sun in the summer, and hide bad hair days year-round.

Just Hats is brimming with both knit and crochet patterns for all levels of expertise. The patterns come in a variety of styles suitable for men, women, and children. Basic embellishments like tassels and pom-poms make personal statements on even the simplest of hats. Adding fancy yarns or stitch variety further personalizes your chapeau.

There are eight chapters in this book, each with a specific focus. New knitters will want to start with the simpler patterns in the beginning and then move their way toward the more advanced patterns in the later chapters, which feature instructions for techniques like granny squares (chapter four), color patterning (chapter six), and felting (chapter seven). Easy patterns are included in every section, so if you know the basics, feel free to jump from chapter to chapter.

We assume you know the basic knitting skills of knit and purl, and the basic crochet skills of single crochet, double crochet, and half double crochet. If you need to learn these basic stitches or refresh your memory, there are a number of free resources. Learntoknit.com and learntocrochet.com offer good introductions to first-time stitchers. Crochet.about.com and knitting.about.com provide tutorials on more advanced techniques and forums for asking questions of on-staff experts. Also, most libraries have good knitting and crochet reference books.

This book follows the standards and guidelines created by the Craft Yarn Council of America to help you choose patterns that are right for your skill level. Each pattern is labeled as **beginner, easy, intermediate,** or **experienced**. **Beginner** patterns are suitable for first-time knitters and crocheters and only require basic stitch skills. **Easy** patterns call for basic stitches, repetitive pattern work, simple color changes, simple shaping, and finishing. **Intermediate** patterns include a variety of stitches and techniques such as lacework, simple intarsia, double-pointed needles, and finishing. Projects using advanced techniques such as short rows, multicolor changes, complicated cables, lace patterns, detailed shaping, finishing, and using fine threads are for **experienced** knitters and crocheters.

KNOWING YOUR YARNS

In today's marketplace there is a dazzling array of yarns. Knowing the inherent qualities of each type of yarn will lead you to pleasing results when you experiment with different texture combinations.

Traditional **smooth** yarns give good stitch definition and are great for trying different stitches or experimenting with color. In a variety of gauges from super fine to super bulky, these yarns come in a wide range of fibers and blends to fit any project or budget.

Brushed yarns give off a "halo" of hair-like fiber and work well on large needles and hooks in simple stitches. They include mohair, mohair blends, angora, and synthetic yarns.

Chenille yarn looks and feels like velvet. It is best to knit and crochet these yarns at a firm gauge.

Other yarns are **heavily textured.** Bouclés, for instance, are a "loopy" yarn, which can help to hide a multitude of stitching sins. They are best used on larger needles and hooks. They work up fast, but be careful: make sure to pick up the entire thread and not to catch your needle or hook on the "loop" part of the yarn only.

Embellishing a hat with **eyelash yarns** is a fun way to express your inner diva. Since the "lash" part of the yarn is often connected by a thin thread, eyelash yarns can easily be worked with other yarns to great effect.

A good rule of thumb with any fancy or textured yarn is "less is more." Save the fancy stitchwork for smoother yarns. Let the dazzling yarn do the work for you!

FINDING YOUR GAUGE

Getting your gauge may be a new concept if you haven't been knitting or crocheting very long. In general, gauge (sometimes called tension) is the number of stitches and rows measured over a number of inches (or centimeters) of your fabric. Every knitter or crocheter has her or his own particular tension **even when using the same needles and yarn as another person,** so it is important to make sure you get an accurate gauge in order to make a hat that will match the size in the pattern.

You need to knit or crochet a gauge swatch to find your gauge number, or "G" number. As a starting place, use the needle or hook size recommended by the manufacturer, which can be found on the yarn label. Needles and hooks are sized in two ways: the actual size measured in millimeters (mm) and a descriptive size. Knitting needles have descriptive sizes that are expressed in numbers and crochet hooks have descriptive sizes that are expressed in letters. For example, 5 mm knitting needles are size 8 and 5 mm crochet hooks are size H.

Knit or crochet a swatch in the stitch called for by your project that is AT LEAST 4" (10 cm) wide. With a ruler, count the number of stitches in a 4" (10 cm) width (including half-stitches if there are any). Divide this number by 4, and you have your "G" number, or THE NUMBER OF STITCHES PER INCH. It is a good idea to take this measurement at a few different places on the fabric and average them. Your number may have half or quarter stitches represented (as a decimal point if you did your division on a calculator).

If you did not get very close to one of the gauges in the pattern, go up a needle size if your gauge is too tight, or down a needle size if your gauge is too loose, and try again. Finding your gauge accurately is important for a proper fit!

STANDARD YARN WEIGHT SYSTEM
CATEGORIES OF YARN, GAUGE RANGES, AND RECOMMENDED NEEDLE AND HOOK SIZES

YARN WEIGHT SYMBOL & CATEGORY NAMES	1 SUPER FINE	2 FINE	3 LIGHT	4 MEDIUM	5 BULKY	6 SUPER BULKY
TYPE OF YARNS IN CATEGORY	Sock, Fingering, Baby	Sport, Baby	DK, Light Worsted	Worsted, Afghan, Aran	Chunky, Craft, Rug	Bulky, Roving
KNIT GAUGE RANGE* IN STOCKINETTE STITCH TO 4 INCHES	27–32 sts	23–26 sts	21–24 sts	16–20 sts	12–15 sts	6–11 sts
RECOMMENDED NEEDLE IN METRIC SIZE RANGE	2.25–3.25 mm	3.25–3.75 mm	3.75–4.5 mm	4.5–5.5 mm	5.5–8 mm	8 mm and larger
RECOMMENDED NEEDLE U.S. SIZE RANGE	1 to 3	3 to 5	5 to 7	7 to 9	9 to 11	11 and larger
CROCHET GAUGE* RANGES IN SINGLE CROCHET TO 4 INCH	21–32 sts	16–20 sts	12–17 sts	11–14 sts	8–11 sts	5–9 sts
RECOMMENDED HOOK IN METRIC SIZE RANGE	2.25–3.5 mm	3.5–4.5 mm	4.5–5.5 mm	5.5–6.5 mm	6.5–9 mm	9 mm and larger
RECOMMENDED HOOK U.S. SIZE RANGE	B–1 to E–4	E–4 to 7	7 to I–9	I–9 to K–10½	K–10½ to M–13	M–13 and larger

*Guidelines Only: The above reflect the most commonly used gauges and needle or hook sizes for specific yarn categories.

YARN WEIGHTS

When describing yarn as "bulky" or "sportweight," different people mean different things. The Craft Yarn Council of America has established guidelines called the Standard Yarn Weight System to standardize descriptions of yarn thickness. The **materials section** of each pattern in this book features an icon of a skein of yarn with a number on it. That number corresponds to one of these categories. The guiding principle of this system is the smaller the number, the thinner the yarn.

SEAMLESS TECHNIQUES

FOR KNITTERS

If using double-pointed needles, distribute stitches evenly on each needle (see illustration 1-1). Cast on loosely for a more comfortable hat. To avoid twisting the first row at the join, cast on an extra stitch, work the first two rows back and forth, then join the work by knitting the first and last stitch together on the third row.

After you knit the body of the hat, you will decrease at regular intervals to shape the crown. After several decrease rounds, you'll find that you have too few stitches to fit around the circular needle. At this point, switch to double-pointed needles.

There are two methods of decreasing most commonly used. The first technique, called knit 2 together (abbreviated k2tog), is worked as follows: Insert the right needle into the first two stitches on the left needle, wrap the yarn the way you normally would, pulling the yarn through the two stitches (see illustration 2-1). The two

stitches will fall off the needle, leaving one new stitch on the right needle. This is also called a right-slanted decrease because the knit 2 together stitches slant to the right.

To create a left-slanted decrease, patterns often use a technique called slip, slip, knit (abbreviated ssk). This is worked as follows: Insert the right needle tip into the first stitch on the left needle as if you were going to knit it and then slip it to the right needle, slip the second stitch the same way (see illustration 3-1). Insert the tip of the left needle into the front of the two slipped stitches, wrap the yarn around the right needle as you normally would, and knit the two stitches off the needle (see illustration 3-2).

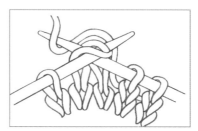
2-1. Knit 2 together.

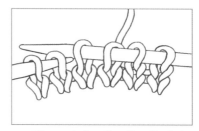
3-1. Slip 2 stitches for slip, slip, knit.

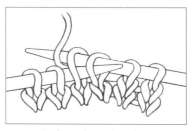
3-2. Knit slipped stitches for slip, slip, knit.

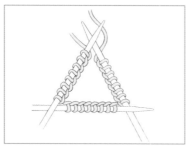
1-1. Using double-pointed needles.

FOR CROCHETERS

Crochet patterns are made in "multiples" that repeat across the row. Often a pattern will contain a multiple of a particular number plus some extra stitches. These extra stitches provide balance in the pattern so your piece will begin and end symmetrically. After you have created the foundation chain it is advisable to use markers between multiples as you set up your pattern.

Crochet patterns increase stitches by working more than one stitch in a space and decrease stitches by working two stitches together. Increase a stitch (shown here in single crochet) by working a stitch into a space and then inserting the hook into the same space (illustration 1-1). Work a second stitch into the same space (illustration 1-2) for one stitch increased (illustration 1-3). On the next row, make single crochets above both stitches.

To decrease, single crochet 2 together by pulling up a loop in one space and then a second loop in the next space (illustration 2-1). Place the yarn over the hook and draw through all 3 loops on the

hook (illustration 2-2). One stitch is decreased (illustration 2-3).

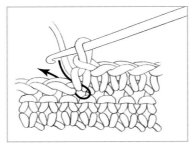

1-1. Increase in single crochet: inserting hook into same space.

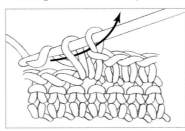

1-2. Working second stitch into a space.

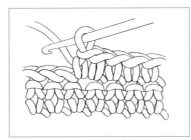

1-3. Increase finished.

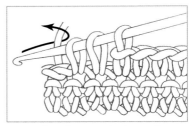

2-1. Pull up loop to single crochet 2 together: in one space, one in next space.

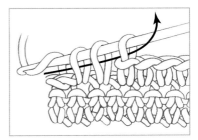

2-2. Yarn over, draw through all 3 loops.

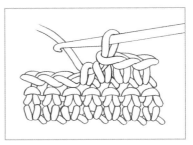

2-3. Decrease finished.

EDGY EDGINGS

For hats constructed from the bottom up, the most important thing to keep in mind is that the edging has to be able to stretch over the entire head and be snug enough that the hat stays on. No matter which edging you choose, make sure your cast-on edge is not too tight. If you tend to cast on tightly, try casting on with a needle or hook that is one or two sizes bigger than you use to make the rest of the hat.

Fold-up brims provide extra warmth. If you choose to make a hat with a brim, keep in mind that the "wrong side" is the side that will show. A reversible stitch such as rib is great because there is no wrong side to the fabric. If the pattern you use is seamed (constructed back and forth, not in the round) remember to sew the brim seam on the outside of the hat so that it will be hidden when the trim is folded over.

If you choose a stitch pattern that has an even number of stitches, while your hat pattern calls for an odd number of stitches, simply increase a stitch on the last row of your edging. It will be virtually invisible. The simplest invisible knit increase is a make one.

SIMPLE KNIT EDGINGS

Rolled Edge: One of the properties of stockinette stitch is that it tends to roll. This provides a nice decorative detail with a minimum amount of work. Cast on the required number of stitches and simply knit (if you are working in the round) or knit a row, purl a row (for a seamed hat) on an extra inch and a half (4 cm) before you begin your pattern.

Garter Stitch Edge: This stitch is very stretchy so use a needle at least 2 needle sizes smaller than you would

for the rest of your hat and knit every row. When working in the round, you must knit 1 row, purl 1 row to achieve the same effect.

Rib Edge: Alternating columns of knit and purl stitches creates a very stretchy fabric (remember to go down a needle size when using this stitch). The simplest rib is 1x1 rib, which is knit 1 stitch, purl 1 stitch. You need to have an even number of stitches and work as follows: **Row 1** Knit 1, purl 1; repeat to end of row. Repeat Row 1 for rib pattern.

Another common rib pattern is 2x2 rib, which is worked over a multiple of 4 stitches: **Row 1** Knit 2, purl 2; repeat to end of row. Repeat Row 1 for rib pattern.

Seed Stitch Edge: This rib variation is unlike other ribbing because instead of knitting the knit stitches and purling the purl stitches, you alternate knit and purl stitches each row. Over an odd number of stitches: **Row 1** *Knit 1, purl 1; repeat from * to last stitch, end knit 1. Repeat Row 1 for pattern.

SIMPLE CROCHET EDGES

Since crocheting provides a denser fabric than knitting does, it is not as important for the edging to pull in the rest of the hat. The chain row at the bottom of the hat is an excellent base for many edgings. For a simple, smooth finish, slip stitch around the chain-base after you have completed your hat.

Double Crochet Ribbed Brim: This finish makes a somewhat bulky, slightly elastic ribbing to be turned up to the outside. Working a double crochet around the front post of the stitch below makes the double crochet pop forward, around the back post makes it recede. This ribbing is worked in rounds the same as the body, and requires an even number of stitches. After your hat reaches the required length, slip stitch in the beginning of the round to join. Turn.

Round 1 With wrong side facing, chain 2. If your hat has an even number of stitches, skip the first post right after the beginning chain and begin with the next post. If your hat has an odd number of stitches, begin with the first post right after the beginning chain. Double crochet around the front post of the appropriate single crochet, [back post double crochet next single crochet, front post double crochet next single crochet] around. The last front post double crochet should be in the same single crochet as the slip stitch of the previous turning. Slip stitch in the top of the turning chain.

Round 2 Chain 2, front post double crochet each front post double crochet, back post double crochet each back post double crochet around, slip stitch in the top of the turning chain.

Repeat Round 2 for desired length of ribbed brim, generally 4" to 5" (10 to 13 cm). Fasten off.

Single Crochet Ribbed Brim: This is the more complicated of the two crocheted brim variations offered here. After you've worked your hat to the required length, slip stitch in the beginning of the round. Turn.

Row 1 Chain the number of stitches according to your gauge for 1" (2.5 cm) for narrow brim, 4" to 5" (10 to 13 cm) for wide brim. Single crochet in the 2nd chain from the hook, single crochet in each chain to body, skip single crochet of join, slip stitch in the next 2 single crochet of body. Turn.

Row 2 Skip slip stitches, single crochet through the back loop (single crochet through back loop) in each single crochet across. Turn.

Row 3 Chain 1, single crochet through the back loop of each single crochet across, skip single crochet of join, slip stitch through both loops in the next 2 single crochet of body. Turn.

Repeat Rows 2 and 3 around hat.

If your hat has an even number of stitches, end with a Row 3, then end row with a slip stitch in the last single crochet of body.

If your hat has an odd number of stitches, end with a Row 2, at the outer edge of the ribbing.

Join ends of ribbing by seaming or slip stitch.

To attach a narrow brim that doesn't fold upward when worn, *with right sides together,* hold the last row of ribbing together with the beginning chain of ribbing and sew the brim to the hat with whipstitch, or a crochet slip stitch seam, carefully matching stitches.

To attach a wide brim that is folded upward when worn, place *wrong sides together,* then follow instructions for narrow brim.

Picot Border: Picots add an Andean touch to ear-flaps and flirty flair to basic edges. There are many variations of picot. Here is a simple example: In the same stitch work [3 double crochet, chain 3, slip stitch in 3rd chain from the hook, 3 double crochet].

Picot Edging: Single crochet in one space, *[skip the next space, picot in the next space, skip the next space, single crochet in the next space]; repeat from * around the hat. Join the round with a slip stitch in top of the starting chain-3. Fasten off.

FUN FINISHES

Even the simplest hat becomes a masterpiece when you embellish it. These techniques will help you personalize any pattern you choose to make.

CROCHET CORKSCREWS

Make a chain the desired length. Double crochet in 3rd chain from hook, work 2 more double crochet in the same chain, 3 double crochet in each chain to the end. Cut yarn, leaving tail for sewing. Pull the yarn tail through the last double crochet to secure.

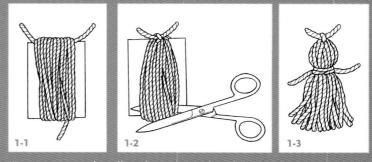

Wrap yarn around cardboard, cut one end, and tie tassel.

TASSELS

Tassels add a dramatic finish to just about any hat. To make a tassel, cut a piece of cardboard the length you want the finished tassel. Wrap the yarn around the cardboard (see illustration 1-1), remembering that more strands make a fuller, heavier tassel. Slip a piece of yarn under one end and tie in a knot. Cut the other end open (see illustration 1-2). With a separate piece of yarn, wrap and tie the tassel near the top (see illustration 1-3).

ROPE CORDS

Cut 6 strands of yarn, each approximately 94" (238.5 cm) long. (If you are using a bulky yarn for the tie, you may want to use fewer than 6 yarn strands to make the cord.) Hold lengths together and tie a knot at each end. Anchor one end and twist the other end clockwise many times until the piece is very tight and almost kinked. Hold the rope cord in the center and release both ends, allowing them to wrap around each other.

POM-POMS

Pom-poms are not just for ski hats. They can be big or little, multicolored or solid. To make, cut a piece of cardboard the size of the finished pom-pom and wrap the yarn tightly around the cardboard until the cardboard is completely covered (see illustration 2-1). Slide the yarn from the cardboard and tie tightly around the middle. Cut loops at both ends (see illustration 2-2). Trim pom-pom if necessary (see illustration 2-3).

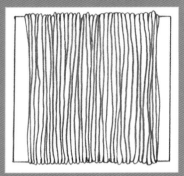

2-1. Wrap yarn around cardboard.

2-2. Cut loops at both ends.

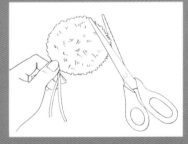

2-3. Trim the pom-pom.

EMBELLISHMENTS

We have included knit and crochet instructions for flowers. However, the possibilities are endless.

CROCHET FLOWERS

Chain 4. Join with slip stitch to form a ring.

Round 1 Chain 1 (counts as 1 single crochet), work 11 single crochet into the ring. Join the round with slip stitch in chain-1.

Round 2 [Chain 3, skip the next stitch, single crochet in the next stitch] 6 times—6 chain-3 loops.

Round 3 [In the next chain-3 loop work (single crochet, half double crochet, 3 double crochet, half double crochet, single crochet)] 6 times. Join the round with a slip stitch in the first single crochet. Fasten off.

KNIT FLOWERS

Cast on 42 stitches.

Row 1 (wrong side) Purl.

Row 2 Knit 2, *knit 1, slip this stitch back to the left needle, lift the next 5 stitches on the left needle over this stitch and off the needle, yarn over twice, knit the first stitch again, knit 2; repeat from *—27 stitches.

Row 3 Purl 1, *purl 2 together, drop 1 of the yarn-over loops, (knit into the front and back) twice in remaining yarn over of previous row, purl 1; repeat from * to last stitch, purl 1—32 stitches.

Row 4 Knit 1, *knit 3 together; repeat from *, end knit 1—12 stitches.

Row 5 *Purl 2 together; repeat from *—6 stitches; slip 2nd, 3rd, 4th, 5th, and 6th stitches over the first stitch. Fasten off and sew seam.

Make another flower if desired. Use contrasting color to attach the flower to the hat.

EMBROIDERY

Running Stitch: This basic sewing stitch looks fresh and new when made with yarn on knitted or crocheted fabric. Use a blunt, large-eyed needle and insert it into the fabric from the wrong side to the right side, leaving a 3" (7.5 cm) tail of yarn to weave in later. Insert the needle back to the wrong side and be careful not to pull the yarn too tightly or it will distort the fabric. Continue the running stitch for desired length.

Chain Stitch is a simple embroidery technique that looks great on knitted and crocheted fabric because it mimics the shape of the stitches (see Vintage Vines, page 48). Once mastered, it is easy to "draw" with this method either following a chart or working freeform. Personalize a simple hat by embroidering the recipient's initials.

Choose a yarn smooth enough to glide through the finished fabric.
Step 1: Using a blunt, large-eyed yarn needle, secure the yarn by gently attaching it to a stitch on the wrong side of work. Leave a 3" (7.5 cm) tail for weaving in.

Step 2: Draw the needle through to the right side of work.
Step 3: Create a small loop by inserting the needle back where it came out. Secure the loop with your finger. Pull the needle through, above the loop, creating a chain stitch (see illustration). Do not pull too tightly or fabric will warp.

Repeat Step 3 in any direction as desired, careful to space chain stitches evenly.

Blanket Stitch, sometimes called buttonhole stitch, is a great finishing touch on edges. (See page 33).
Step 1: Using a blunt, large-eyed yarn needle, secure the yarn by gently attaching it to a stitch on the wrong side of your work. Leave a 3" (7.5 cm) tail to weave in later.
Step 2: Carefully draw the yarn needle through to the right side of work, close to the edge.
Step 3: Bring the needle above the yarn and insert it a couple of stitches to the right of where you first inserted it (see illustration).
Step 4: Pull the needle past the edge of the hat to complete the stitch.

Repeat Steps 3 and 4, inserting the needle the same number of stitches apart for even spacing.

Running Stitch.

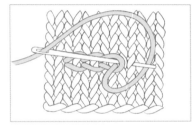

Chain stitch.

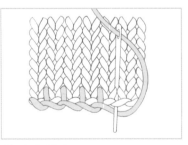

Blanket Stitch.

NEEDLES AND HOOKS

As you become more experienced as a knitter or crocheter, you will develop a preference for a certain type of needle and hook. Needles and hooks range from plastic and metal to bamboo and exotic woods like ebony—some are gold plated! Use whatever makes you most comfortable. Sometimes it is beneficial to knit back and forth on circular needles (instead of straight needles) because the cord connecting the needles can accommodate more stitches.

OTHER TOOLS

Scissors and a tape measure are a must. It is handy to have a large-eyed, blunt needle for finishing and weaving in ends. You also might find it useful to have stitch markers and cable needles close at hand.

THE EASIEST HATS EVER

These knit and crochet hats are super-simple and can be made in multiple sizes, in multiple gauges. They are just rectangles that are joined after stitching. If you can make a swatch, you are halfway there to making these hats. On the following page, we teach you how to sew the sides together. Simply pick your size, pick your yarn, and GO. Add a distinctive brim and finishing trim to make a hat just the way you want it!

PICKING YOUR SIZE

Once you have your gauge, or "G" number (see page 8), decide which size hat you want to make. While approximate ages are given for the hat sizes at the beginning of each pattern, all heads are unique! It is best to measure and pick the size according to the Finished Circumference measurements. Keep in mind that both knitted and crocheted fabrics stretch. For a snug fit, choose a size that is 2" (5 cm) smaller than the head for which it is intended. For a looser fit, match the hat size to the head.

READING THE CHARTS

When you come to a chart in your pattern, look for the size you wish to make, which is found **across the row,** from smallest to largest. The "G" numbers appear down the side, in stitches per inch. Find your "G" number along the left side, then follow across the row of numbers to find your size. For instance, if you are making a hat in G3 in size Child M, look down the column to G3, and then across to Child M and cast on 55 sts. If

there is only one column of numbers, it applies to all sizes. If there is only one row of numbers, it applies to all gauges.

FINISHING

Once you're done stitching, you'll need to sew the hat. Here are two methods from which to choose.

INVISIBLE SEAM

Line up the piece with the right sides facing out. Attach the yarn at the lower edge. Start on one side and *insert your needle under the running strand between 2 stitches on the outside edge of the opposite side of the work, draw the needle through; repeat from *, and alternate sides as you work up the seam (see illustrations 1-1 and 1-2).

SLIP STITCH SEAM

Work on the wrong side with the right sides of the piece facing each other. With a crochet hook the same size as the needles used, insert the hook through both fabrics, place the yarn over the hook and draw the hook through the seam stitches and the loop on the hook (see illustration 2). Continue to the end.

1-1. Invisible seam—stockinette stitch.

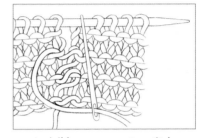

1-2. Invisible seam—garter stitch.

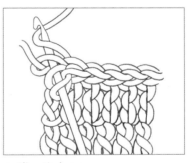

2. Slip stitch seam.

EASY-PEASY KNIT HAT

KNIT/BEGINNER

This basic pattern can be quickly jazzed up with a variety of embellishments.

SIZE

Child: S=6 months–4 years, M/L=6–14 years
Adult: S/M, L
17 (18½, 20½, 22½)" [43 (47, 52, 57) cm] circumference x 6 (7, 7½, 8)" [15 (18, 19, 20.5) cm] depth

MATERIALS

• Approximately 100–200 yd (91.5–183 m) for Child, 200–330 yd (183–302 m) for Adult. **Yarn amounts will vary due to hat size and yarn gauge.**

• 1 pair straight needles in size necessary to obtain gauge

• Large-eyed, blunt needle

GAUGE

Work your gauge over garter stitch (knit every row), following the instructions under "Finding Your Gauge" on page 8.

HAT

Gauge:	CHILD S	CHILD M/L	ADULT S/M	ADULT L
	Cast on:			
G2 (2 sts per inch)	34	37	41	45 stitches
G2.5	42	46	51	56
G3	51	55	61	68
G3.5	60	65	72	79
G4	68	74	82	90
G4.5	77	83	92	101
G5	85	92	102	112

Work even in garter stitch until piece measures:

	6"	7"	7½"	8"
	15 cm	18 cm	19 cm	20.5 cm

Bind off all stitches loosely.

FINISHING

Sew up back seam (see page 9).

FUN FINISHES

POM-POM POINTS

Make two pom-poms (see instructions, page 14). Pull the pom-pom ties through the hat to the wrong side at the corners, then knot the ties on the wrong side. Weave in ends.

GATHERED AND TIED CORNERS

Make two rope cords (see instructions, page 14). Gather one corner of the hat and tie the rope cord in a bow, knotting the ends where desired, and cutting off excess cord below the knot. Unravel the cord ends. Repeat on other side.

DRAWSTRING TOP

Make one rope cord approximately

120" (305 cm) long (see instructions on page 14), using three strands of yarn. Thread the cord through the hat stitches, approximately 1½" (4 cm) down from the top, starting just left of the center front. Weave the cord in and out from front to back, about every 4–5 stitches, finishing the weaving so the end comes to extra space outside of the hat. Pull both ends gently, creating a drawstring effect, and knot once in the middle. Knot the ends of the rope cord at the desired length and cut off any excess. Make two pom-poms (see directions on page 14), and attach them to the ends of the rope cord with the pom-pom ties. Weave in ends.

4-CORNERS

Making sure the seam is at the back, sew the top seam starting at the corner, for

CHILD S	CHILD M/L	ADULT S/M	ADULT L
2½"	2¾"	3"	3½"
6.5 cm	7 cm	7.5 cm	9 cm

Flip the work and using a new length of yarn, repeat the seam on the other end. There is now a center, unsewn opening. Switch direction. Hold each unsewn side up to ITSELF, rather than to the other side, and using another length of yarn, close the seam, creating 4 corners.

From left to right: Drawstring top hat in Glitterspun and Fun Fur, pom-pom points in Jiffy Thick & Quick, 4-corners in Homespun.

AS PICTURED

 LION BRAND GLITTERSPUN
60% ACRYLIC, 13% POLYESTER, 27% CUPRO
1¾ OZ (50 G) 115 YD (105 M) BALL

 LION BRAND FUN FUR
100% POLYESTER
SOLID COLORS 1¾ OZ (50 G) 64 YD (58 M) BALL
PRINTS 1½ OZ (40 G) 57 YD (52 M) BALL

LION BRAND JIFFY THICK & QUICK
100% ACRYLIC
5 OZ (140 G) 84 YD (76 M) BALL

LION BRAND HOMESPUN
98% ACRYLIC, 2% POLYESTER
6 OZ (170 G) 185 YD (167 M) SKEIN

EASY-PEASY CROCHET HAT

CROCHET/BEGINNER

The versatility of this pattern will have you returning to these pages again and again.

SIZE

Note These sizes are *suggestions only*. Since this hat is crocheted from side to side, you can work exactly to the desired head measurements.
Child: S=6–36 months,
M=3–5 years, L=5–14 years
Adult: S/M, L
18 (19, 20, 21, 23)" [45.5 (48.5, 51, 53.5, 58.5) cm] *or desired circumference* x 6½ (7, 7½, 8, 9)" [16.5 (18, 19, 20.5, 23) cm] *or desired length*

MATERIALS

• Approximately 100–200 yd (91.5–183 m) for Child, 200–330 yd (183–302 m) for Adult. **Yarn amounts will vary due to hat size and yarn gauge**

• Crochet hook in size necessary to obtain gauge

• Stitch markers

• Large-eyed, blunt needle

GAUGE

A pre-measured gauge is not necessary; however, see instructions on page 8 for general gauge and charted pattern instructions.

NOTES

• Hat is worked from *side to side;* in other words, the number of stitches that you begin with makes up the height of the hat, and the length that you make the piece becomes the circumference of the hat. Therefore, this hat can be made with any yarn, and custom fit to the desired head!

• Some of the Fun Finishes require shorter or longer hat heights (the number of stitches you begin with). Before you start your hat, look at the Fun Finishes to see if your desired finish requires a particular height.

• Working the first row of single crochet into the *back* of the foundation chain (inserting the hook into the nub on the back of the chain, rather than into the loops on the front) will make for a neater finished seam.

HAT

Loosely make a chain that measures the desired depth (see Note about depths for desired finishing), or approximately:

CHILD S	CHILD M	CHILD L
6½"	7"	7½"
16.5 cm	18 cm	19 cm

ADULT S/M	ADULT L
8"	9"
20.5 cm	23 cm

Chain 3.
Row 1 Single crochet in the back of the 2nd chain from the hook (see Note above), single crochet in the

back of each chain to the desired depth, or length chosen above, measured without stretching. If you do not need all of the chains to achieve the depth, ignore any extras. Mark this side as the right side. Turn.

Row 2 Chain 1, single crochet in each single crochet across. Turn. (**Note** As you continue to work, check the depth measurement occasionally to make sure you are working on target.) Repeat Row 2 until the rectangle, slightly stretched, measures the desired head circumference or:

18"	19"	20"	21"	23"
45.5 cm	48.5 cm	51 cm	53.5 cm	58.5 cm

End the rectangle by working a right side row—an odd number of rows will have been worked. Cut yarn, leaving a tail long enough for sewing, approximately 24" (61 cm). Pull yarn tail through the last loop to fasten. Thread tail onto a large-eyed, blunt needle.

FINISHING

Sew the back seam (short side of rectangle) as follows: Hold the rectangle so the top loops of the beginning chain lie in front going in one direction, and the top loops of the last row lie behind and face the opposite direction. Whipstitch the two sides together through both thicknesses, matching the loops as follows: Insert the needle under 2 loops at front and under 2 loops at back, draw the yarn through to the back, bring the needle to the front, then move to the next stitch. Do not over-tighten. Do not fasten end yet, you may need to

From left to right: Watchcap with self brim and gathered top in Cotton-Ease, flat seam with points and crochet corkscrews in Color Waves, natty cap with folded top and self brim in Jiffy, scrunchy in Landscapes, flat seam with ears in Wool-Ease.

continue with it. Remove any extra beginning chains, fasten off, and weave in all ends to wrong side of work.

TOP CLOSINGS

The Fun Finishes either use one of the top closings below, or have other instructions. Decide which Fun Finish you want and use the appropriate top closing.

FLAT SEAM

Flatten hat tube with the top edges even; the side seam and yarn end should be held in your right hand. Continue to whipstitch evenly across top edge through both thicknesses, matching rows by inserting needle under 2 loops at front, then under 2 loops at back, drawing the yarn through to back, and bringing the sewing needle to the front. Fasten off. Leave the seam on the outside of hat for more angular points, or turn inside out for subtler points.

GATHERED TOP

Continuing with threaded needle, weave yarn in and out through every other row of top edge as follows: Insert needle under edge stitch of first row, draw yarn to back, skip the next row. From the back, insert the needle under the edge stitch of the next row, draw the yarn to front, skip the next row. Continue in this way to the end of the seam. Pull yarn to tighten and gather stitches. Fasten off securely.

Note on Gathering: If your yarn is extremely thick or tends to break, either choose a different closing *or* use a thinner, sturdier yarn in a coordinating color for gathering.

FUN FINISHES

Three of the Fun Finishes below are added to a completed Easiest Hat. **For the Self-brim and the Scrunchy you must plan ahead and make the hat longer.**

EARS (AS SHOWN ON PAGE 23, WOOL-EASE #176 SPRING GREEN, 18".)

Finish hat with Flat Seam. Each ear is the triangle portion of the corner, stitched around and tightened to gather. Flatten hat. With threaded yarn needle, starting at one edge approximately 2" (5 cm) down from corner, weave yarn in and out of the top layer of hat rows, working diagonally across the corner, then continuing across the back layer to the beginning. Pull the ends of the woven yarn to gather, knot, and weave in yarn tails. Repeat on other side.

POINTS (AS SEEN ON PAGE 23, COLORWAVES #307 CARIBBEAN, 22" [56 CM])

Finish hat with Flat Seam. Wear as is or sew trims to the points; such as tassels (see page 14) or corkscrews (see page 14).

FOLDED TOP (AS SEEN ON PAGE 23)

Finish hat with Flat Seam. Find and mark the center of the top seam. Continuing with threaded yarn needle, tack the two side points to the center. Fasten securely. If desired, sew trim to top; either a pom-pom (see page 14), flower (see page 15), or a button.

STRING TIE (NOT PICTURED)

Do not finish top. After seaming the side, fasten. Use self-string (instructions below) or ribbon to gather the top as follows: Weave one end in and out of edge stitches every other row of top edge. Pull end to gather, then knot securely. Tie a bow if desired.

SELF BRIM (AS SEEN ON PAGE 23, NATTY CAP SAMPLE IN JIFFY #173 GRASS GREEN, 23" [58.5 CM] CIRCUMFERENCE WITH 3" [7.5 CM] SELF BRIM AND FOLDED TOP, AND ALSO ON PAGE 23, WATCHCAP SAMPLE IN COTTON-EASE #148 POPSICLE BLUE, 19" [48.5 CM] CIRCUMFERENCE WITH 3" [7.5 CM] SELF BRIM AND GATHERED TOP.)

Must be planned before beginning Easy-Peasy Hat. Make the beginning chain 3" (7.5 cm) longer than given for size, or even longer, allowing enough height to turn upward and use as a brim. Continue with hat instruction as written.

SCRUNCHY (AS SEEN ON PAGE 23, SCRUNCHY IN LANDSCAPES #277 COUNTRY SUNSET, 20" [51 CM].)

Must be planned before beginning Easy-Peasy Hat. Make the beginning chain 2½" (6.5 cm) longer than measurement given for size. Continue with hat instructions as written. After seaming the side, drop the sewing tail. Thread needle with another length of yarn. Gather the hat 2½" (6.5 cm) down from the top edge, weaving the end in and out of every other row around the hat. Pull yarn tightly to gather, secure the tails. Pick up the dropped sewing tail and gather, the top edge stitches same as for the gathered top above, except do not pull the top completely closed. Pull approximately ⅔ of the way and secure the tails. Turn the top to the outside to shape like the "scrunchy" hair accessory (see Note on gathering under Gathered Top, previous page).

TRIMS

SELF-STRING

Use to gather the top edge. Make a chain 20" (51 cm) long for the knot ends, 26" (66 cm) or longer for bow. Slip stitch in the 2nd chain from the hook, then slip stitch in each chain to the end, fasten off, and weave ends.

CORKSCREWS—MAKE 2 (DIRECTIONS ON PAGE 14)

Sew Corkscrew to each point. Twist to desired effect.

AS PICTURED

 LION BRAND COTTON-EASE
50% COTTON, 50% ACRYLIC
3½ OZ (100 G) 207 YD (189 M) BALL

 LION BRAND COLOR WAVES
83% ACRYLIC, 17% POLYESTER
3 OZ (85 G) 125 YD (114 M) SKEIN

 LION BRAND JIFFY
100% ACRYLIC
SOLID COLORS: 3 OZ (85 G)
135 YD (123 M) BALL

 LION BRAND LANDSCAPES
50% WOOL, 50% ACRYLIC
1¾ OZ (50 G) 55 YD (50 M) BALL

 LION BRAND WOOL-EASE
80% ACRYLIC, 20% WOOL
3 OZ (85 G) 197 YD (180 M) BALL

2.

SEAMLESS HATS

Knitting and crocheting in the round have many advantages. There is no seam, which means less finishing for you and a more comfortable hat for the wearer. Also, the right side is always facing so you can watch the hat develop as you work. Knitting in the round minimizes purling, which, for many knitters, means they can work faster and more comfortably.

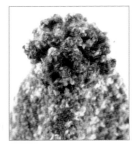

BASIC CROCHET HAT

CROCHET/EASY

Crocheting a seamless hat is tons of fun—you just start at the top and go around and around.

SIZE

Child: S=6–36 months, M=3–6 years, L=6–16 years
Adult: S/M, L
17–18 (19–20, 20–21, 21–22, 23–24)" [43–45.5 (48.5–51, 51–53.5, 53.5–56, 58.5–61) cm] circumference x 6 (6½, 7, 7½, 8½)" [15 (16.5, 18, 19, 21.5) cm] depth

MATERIALS

• Approximately 100–200 yd (91.5–183 m) for Child, 200–330 yd (183–302 m for Adult). **Yarn amounts will vary due to hat size and yarn gauge**

• Crochet hook in size necessary to obtain gauge

• Stitch marker

GAUGE

Work your gauge over single crochet, following instructions under "Finding Your Gauge" on page 8.

NOTES

• If you want to make the Top-Knot Topper, read the instructions on page 28 before you begin.

CROWN

Make a slip knot, chain 2.
Round 1 Work 6 single crochet in the 2nd chain from the hook. Place marker and continue working in the round; move marker up as you go.
Round 2 Work 2 single crochet in each single crochet around—12 stitches total.
Round 3 [Single crochet in the next single crochet, 2 single crochet in the next single crochet] 6 times around—18 stitches total.
Round 4 [Single crochet in the next 2 single crochet, 2 single crochet in the next single crochet] 6 times around—24 stitches total.
Continue in this way, increasing 6 stitches each round, for the total number of rounds indicated on the chart on page 28 (the number on the chart includes the 4 rounds worked above). **Note** If your "G"/Size calls for a +3 round, then after completing the number of rounds listed, work one more round increasing only 3 stitches (see +3 Round below chart). If your "G"/Size does not call for a +3 round, begin the Body instructions.

+3 ROUND

Work as if you were doing the next increase round, except make only one single crochet instead of 2 in the position of the first increase, work 2nd increase as usual, make only 1 single crochet in the position of the 3rd increase, work 4th increase as usual, make only 1 single crochet in the position of the 5th increase, work 6th increase as usual. Only 3 stitches have been increased on this round.

	CHILD S	CHILD M	CHILD L	ADULT S/M	ADULT L
G1.5	4 rounds+3	5 rounds	5 rounds	5 rounds+3	6 rounds
	(27 stitches)	(30 stitches)	(30 stitches)	(33 stitches)	(36 stitches)
G1.75	5 rounds	5 rounds+3	6 rounds	6 rounds+3	7 rounds
	(30 stitches)	(33 stitches)	(36 stitches)	(39 stitches)	(42 stitches)
G2	6 rounds	6 rounds+3	7 rounds	7 rounds	8 rounds
	(36 stitches)	(39 stitches)	(42 stitches)	(42 stitches)	(48 stitches)
G2.5	7 rounds+3	8 rounds	8 rounds+3	9 rounds	10 rounds
	(45 stitches)	(48 stitches)	(51 stitches)	(54 stitches)	(60 stitches)
G3	9 rounds	9 rounds+3	10 rounds	10 rounds+3	11 rounds+3
	(54 stitches)	(57 stitches)	(60 stitches)	(63 stitches)	(69 stitches)
G3.5	10 rounds+3	11 rounds+3	12 rounds	12 rounds+3	13 rounds+3
	(63 stitches)	(69 stitches)	(72 stitches)	(75 stitches)	(81 stitches)
G4.5	13 rounds+3	14 rounds+3	15 rounds	16 rounds	17 rounds+3
	(81 stitches)	(87 stitches)	(90 stitches)	(96 stitches)	(105 stitches)

BODY

Moving marker up at the beginning of each round, single crochet in each single crochet around until piece measures:

6"	6½"	7"	7½"	8½"
15 cm	16.5 cm	18 cm	19 cm	21.5 cm

Be sure to measure the hat from Round 1 to edge.

FINISHING

Pick from the Edgings and Toppers that follow. Remember to fasten off and weave in ends when you're done.

TOPPERS

TOP KNOT (AS SEEN OPPOSITE)

MUST BE WORKED BEFORE HAT IS BEGUN. Begin basic hat and work Round 1 of Crown. Single crochet in rounds of 6 single crochet, making a tube approximately 4" (10 cm) long. Work Round 2 of Crown. Single crochet 1 round even on 12 single crochet. Continue with Basic Hat pattern. Weave in your tails to wrong side, and tie the top of the tube with an overhand knot.

SELF POM-POM (AS SEEN OPPOSITE)

Make slip knot, leaving a long tail for sewing.

Round 1 Chain 2, work 8 single crochet in 2nd chain from hook, slip stitch in beginning single crochet.

Round 2 Chain 5 (half double crochet, chain 3) 4 times in the first single crochet, (half double crochet, chain 3) 5 times in each single crochet around, slip stitch in 2nd chain of beginning chain. Fasten off. Use the starting tail to sew the pom-pom to the top of hat.

From left to right: Slip stitch brim and self pom-pom in Lion Bouclé, single crochet ribbing in Magic Stripes, top knot and rolled brim in Wool-Ease, and double crochet rib brim in Wool-Ease doubled.

EDGINGS

SLIP STITCH EDGE (AS SEEN ABOVE)

Continuing with right side facing, slip stitch in each single crochet around, adjusting tension for fit. Slip stitch in the beginning single crochet of round.

ROLLED BRIM (AS SEEN ABOVE)

Single crochet around THROUGH FRONT LOOP ONLY until brim measures approximately 1¼" (3.25 cm), or long enough for the edge to curl up on itself. TURN. With wrong side of work facing, slip stitch through both loops of each single crochet to end of wrong side, then slip stitch in beginning of round.

DOUBLE CROCHET RIB BRIM (AS SEEN ABOVE)

When Basic Hat reaches required length, slip stitch in the beginning of round. TURN.

Round 1 With wrong side of hat facing, chain 2. If your hat has an even number of stitches already, skip the first post right after the beginning chain, begin with the next post. If your hat has an odd number of stitches, begin with the first post right after the beginning chain. Double crochet around the front post of the appropriate single crochet. [Back post double crochet next single crochet, front post double crochet next single crochet] around. The last front post double crochet should be in the same single crochet as the slip stitch of the previous turning. Slip stitch in top of the turning-chain to close round.

Round 2 Chain 2, front post double crochet in each front post double crochet, back post double crochet in each back post double crochet around, slip stitch in top of turning-chain to close round.

Repeat Round 2 for desired length of trim.

EASY KNIT HAT

KNIT/EASY

Seemingly endless possibilities spring from this pattern. Once you figure out your gauge, you can mix and match different brim edges with various embellishments.

SIZE

Child: S=6 months–4 years, Child M/L=6–14 years
Adult: S/M, L
16¾ (18½, 20½, 22½)" [42.5 (47, 52, 57) cm] circumference x 6 (7, 7½, 8)" [15 (18, 19, 20.5) cm] depth

MATERIALS

- Approximately 100–200 yds (91.5–183 m) for Child, 200–330 yd (183–302 m) for Adult. **Yarn amounts will vary due to hat size and yarn gauge.**

- 16" (40.5 cm) circular needle and set of 4 or 5 double pointed needles in size necessary to obtain gauge

- Stitch marker

- Large-eyed, blunt needle

GAUGE

Work your gauge over stockinette stitch (knit every round), following instructions under "Finding Your Gauge" on page 8.

BRIM

- If you are working Seed Stitch Edge and your size below is an odd number of stitches, cast on one stitch fewer than below, and increase one stitch on the last round of the seed stitch.

- If you are working Rib Edge, do not cast on the number below, cast on number shown on chart under Rib Edge, and follow those directions.

Gauge With circular needle, cast on:	CHILD S	CHILD M/L	ADULT S/M	ADULT L
G2.5 (2.5 st per inch)	42	46	52	56 stitches
G3	50	56	62	68
G3.5	59	65	72	79
G4	67	74	82	90
G4.5	75	83	92	101
G5	84	92	102	112
G6	100	111	123	135

Join, being careful not to twist, and place marker to mark the beginning of the round or begin as per note on page 10 Work desired edge below, then proceed to hat instructions.

SEED STITCH EDGE

Round 1 *Knit 1, purl 1; repeat from * around—see Note above about cast-on stitches.

Round 2 Purl the knit stitches and knit the purl stitches.

Repeat last round to desired length or approximately:

¾"	1"	1½"	2"
2 cm	2.5 cm	4 cm	5 cm

If you cast on one stitch fewer than shown above for your size, be sure to increase one stitch on the last round.

RIB EDGE

With circular needle, cast on:

G2.5	40	44	52	56 stitches
G3	48	56	60	68
G3.5	56	64	72	76
G4	64	72	80	88
G4.5	72	80	92	100
G5	84	92	100	112
G6	100	108	120	132

Join, being careful not to twist the stitches, and place a marker to mark the beginning of the round.

Round 1 *Knit 2, purl 2; repeat from * around. Continue working the rib pattern in rounds to the desired length, or approximately:

1"	1½"	2"	2"
2.5 cm	4 cm	5 cm	5 cm

From left to right: Flower patch with rolled edge and crocheted flowers in Wool-Ease, stitch in time with running stitch and pom-pom in Wool-Ease Thick & Quick and Kool Wool, rib edge with defining edge and tassel in Color Waves and Landscapes

Next Round Change to stockinette stitch and increase the following number of stitches around:

G2.5	2	2	0	0
G3	2	0	2	0
G3.5	3	1	0	3
G4	3	2	2	2
G4.5	3	3	0	1
G5	0	0	2	0
G6	0	3	3	3

You should now have the same number of stitches as the chart on page 30. Proceed to hat instructions.

GARTER STITCH EDGE

Round 1 Knit.

Round 2 Purl.

Repeat the last 2 rounds until piece measures desired length, or approximately:

¾"	¾"	1"	1½"
2 cm	2 cm	2.5 cm	4 cm

ROLLED EDGE

Work in rounds of stockinette stitch until piece measures approximately 1½" (4 cm).

HAT

Work in rounds of stockinette stitch until piece measures from bottom of Rib, Seed Stitch, Garter Stitch, or Rolled Edge (allowing bottom to roll before measuring).

G2.5	2½" 6.5 cm	3½" 9 cm	4" 10 cm	4½" 11.5 cm
G3	3" 7.5 cm	4" 10 cm	4½" 11.5 cm	5" 12.5 cm
G3.5	3¼" 8.5 cm	4¼" 11 cm	4¾" 12 cm	5¼" 13.5 cm
G4	3¼" 8.5 cm	4¼" 11 cm	4¾" 12 cm	5¼" 13.5 cm
G4.5	3½" 9 cm	4½" 11.5 cm	5" 12.5 cm	5½" 14 cm
G5	3½" 9 cm	4½" 11.5 cm	5" 12.5 cm	5½" 14 cm
G6	4" 10 cm	5" 12.5 cm	5½" 14 cm	6" 15 cm

SHAPE TOP

Note Change to double-pointed needles when there are too few stitches to fit on the circular needle.

Next Round *Knit 2 together, knit 3; repeat from * around. The number of stitches remaining will be:

G2.5	33	37	41	45
G3	40	45	49	54
G3.5	47	52	57	63
G4	53	59	65	72
G4.5	60	66	73	81
G5	67	73	81	89
G6	80	89	98	108

Work 3 rounds even.

Next Round *Knit 2 together, knit 2; repeat from * around as many times as possible. The number of stitches remaining will be:

G2.5	25	28	31	34
G3	30	34	37	40
G3.5	35	39	43	47
G4	40	44	49	54
G4.5	45	49	55	61
G5	50	55	61	67
G6	60	67	73	81

Work 3 rounds even.

G2.5: Next Round *Knit 2 together, knit 1; repeat from * around.

All other gauges: Next Round *Knit 2 together, knit 2; repeat from * around row.

The number of stitches remaining will be:

G2.5	17	19	21	23
G3	22	25	28	30
G3.5	26	29	32	35
G4	30	33	37	40
G4.5	34	37	41	46
G5	37	41	46	50
G6	45	50	55	61

Work 1 round even.

G2.5: Next Round: *Knit 2 together; repeat from * around.

All other gauges Work 3 rounds even.

Next Round: *Knit 2 together, knit 1; repeat from * around as many times as possible.

The number of stitches remaining will be:

G2.5	9	10	11	12
G3	15	17	19	20
G3.5	17	19	21	23
G4	20	22	25	27
G4.5	23	25	27	31
G5	25	27	31	33
G6	30	33	37	41

G2.5 Go to **FINISHING**
All other gauges Work 1 round even.
Next Round *Knit 2 together; repeat from * around.
The number of stitches remaining will be:

G2.5	—	—	—	—
G3	8	9	10	10
G3.5	9	10	11	12
G4	10	11	13	14
G4.5	12	13	14	16
G5	13	14	16	17
G6	15	17	19	21

FINISHING

Break yarn, thread through remaining stitches, and secure.

FUN FINISHES

STRING O' POMS

Make three pom-poms (see instructions on page 4) and tie together, then sew pom-poms to the top of hat.

FLOWER PATCH (AS SEEN ON PAGE 31.)

Make the desired number of flowers and attach as shown, or as desired. Directions for flowers are on page 15.

DEFINING EDGE (AS SEEN ON PAGE 31.)

Work blanket stitch around the hat brim (see page 16). Make one tassel and braid its cord (see page 14). Attach to the top of hat.

STITCH IN TIME (AS SEEN ON PAGE 31.)

Instructions for pom-pom found on page 14. With large-eyed, blunt needle and contrasting color, work a vertical line using backstitch either right or left of center.

AS PICTURED

 LION BRAND WOOL-EASE
80% ACRYLIC, 20% WOOL
3 OZ (85 G) 197 YD (180 M) BALL

 LION BRAND WOOL-EASE THICK & QUICK
80% ACRYLIC, 20% WOOL
6 OZ (170 G) 108 YD (98 M) BALL

 LION BRAND KOOL WOOL
50% MERINO WOOL, 50% ACRYLIC
1³/₄ OZ (50 G) 60 YD (54 M) BALL

LION BRAND COLOR WAVES
83% ACRYLIC, 17% POLYESTER
3 OZ (85 G) 125 YD (114 M) SKEIN

 LION BRAND LANDSCAPES
50% WOOL, 50% ACRYLIC
1³/₄ OZ (50 G) 55 YD (50 M) BALL

KNIT BERETS

KNIT/EASY

Everyone looks good in a beret. This pattern contains instructions for both child and adult sizes.

SIZE

Child 3–8 years (Adult M)
19½ (21)" [49.5 (53.5) cm] slightly stretched, band circumference x 6 (6½)" [15 (16.5) cm] depth
Note Larger size appears in parentheses. If there is only one number, it applies to both sizes.

MATERIALS

CHILD

 LION BRAND WOOL-EASE
80% ACRYLIC, 20% WOOL
3 OZ (85 G) 197 YD (180 M) BALL

1 ball #125 Camel or color of your choice

- Size 6 (4 mm) 16" (40.5 cm) circular needle *or size to obtain gauge*
- Size 6 (4 mm) double-pointed needles—set of 4 or 5
- Size 4 (3.5 mm) 16" (40.5 cm) circular needle
- Size G-6 (4 mm) crochet hook
- Stitch markers

ADULT

LION BRAND HOMESPUN
98% ACRYLIC, 2% POLYESTER
6 OZ (170 G) 185 YD (167 M) SKEIN

1 skein #312 Edwardian or color of your choice

- Size 10 (6 mm) 16" (40.5 cm) circular needle *or size to obtain gauge*
- Size 10 (6 mm) double-pointed needles—set of 4 or 5
- Size 7 (4.5 mm) 16" (40.5 cm) circular needle
- Size J-10 (6 mm) crochet hook
- Stitch markers

GAUGE

CHILD

19 stitches + 30 rows = 4" (10 cm) over stockinette stitch (knit every round) using larger needle.

ADULT

14 stitches + 20 rows = 4" (10 cm) over stockinette stitch using larger needle. *Be sure to check your gauge.*

HAT

With smaller needle, cast on 90 (72) stitches. Place marker and join, being careful not to twist. Work in rounds of knit 1, purl 1 rib for 1" (2.5 cm). Knit 1 round.
Next (Increase) Round *Knit 14 (11), increase 1 stitch by knitting into the front and back of the next stitch; repeat from * around—96 (78) stitches total.
Next (Increase) Round *Knit 15 (12), increase 1 stitch in the next stitch; repeat from * around—102 (84) stitches total.
Continue in this manner, increasing 6 stitches spaced evenly around every round 3 times more—120 (102) stitches total.
Knit 1 round.
Purl 2 rounds.
Knit 1 round.
Next (Decrease) Round *Knit 18 (15), knit 2 together; repeat from * around—114 (96) stitches total.
Knit 1 round even.

Next (Decrease) Round *Knit 17 (14), knit 2 together; repeat from * around—108 (90) stitches total. Knit 1 round even.

Continue in this manner, decreasing 6 stitches evenly spaced around, then working 1 round even 8 times more—60 (42) stitches. Change to double-pointed needles when there are too few stitches to continue working on circular needle easily.

Next (Decrease) Round Decrease 6 stitches evenly spaced around as established on this round, then every following round until 6 stitches remain.

Next (Decrease) Round [Knit 2 together] 3 times, cut yarn leaving a 12" (30.5 cm) tail. Pull tail through remaining 3 stitches.

FINISHING

With a crochet hook, and using the yarn tail from the previous round, chain 10 (8), fasten off and secure to inside to form a loop. Block hat lightly by dampening and stretching over a plate of similar circumference.

CROCHET BERET

CROCHET/EASY

Simple to make and easy to wear, a beret is the perfect hat for the whole family.

SIZE

Child 3–8 years (Adult M)
19¼ (24") [49 (61) cm] circumference x 6" (6½") [15 (16.5) cm] depth **Note** Larger size appears in parentheses. If there is only one number, it applies to both sizes.

MATERIALS

CHILD

 LION BRAND BABYSOFT
60% ACRYLIC, 40% NYLON
5 OZ (140 G) 459 YD (420 M) BALL

1 ball #111 Navy or color of your choice

• Size G-6 (4 mm) crochet hook *or size to obtain gauge*

• Stitch markers

ADULT

 LION BRAND JIFFY THICK & QUICK
100% ACRYLIC
5 OZ (140 G) 84 YD (76 M) BALL

2 balls #212 Adirondacks or color of your choice

• Size P-15 (10 mm) crochet hook *or size to obtain gauge*

• Stitch markers

GAUGE

CHILD

20 stitches + 22.5 rows = 4" (10 cm) over single crochet.

ADULT

6 stitches + 6.75 rows = 4" (10 cm) over single crochet.
Be sure to check your gauge.

STITCH EXPLANATION

Single crochet 2 together (single crochet decrease) Insert hook into stitch and draw up a loop. Insert hook into the next stitch and draw up a loop. Yarn over, draw through all 3 loops on hook (see page 11).

HAT

Chain 10 (6).

Round 1 Work 6 single crochet in the first chain; the remainder of the chain will form the top loop. Place marker and continue working in the round, moving the marker with each new round.

Round 2 Work 2 single crochet in each single crochet around—12 stitches total.

Round 3 [Single crochet in the next single crochet, 2 single crochet in the next single crochet] 6 times around—18 stitches total.

Round 4 [Single crochet in the next 2 single crochet, 2 single crochet in the next single crochet] 6 times around—24 stitches total.

Round 5 [Single crochet in the next 3 single crochet, 2 single crochet in the next single crochet] 6 times around—30 stitches total.

Continue in this way, increasing 6 stitches each round, 19 (4) times more—144 (54) stitches total.

Next Round Slip stitch around.

Next Round Single crochet around, working through the back loop only.

Next (Decrease) Round *Single crochet in the next 22 (7) stitches, single crochet 2 together; repeat from * around—138 (48) stitches total.

Next (Decrease) Round *Single crochet in the next 21 (6) stitches, decrease 1 stitch over the next 2 stitches; repeat from * around—132 (42) stitches total.

Continue in this way, decreasing 6 stitches spaced evenly every round 6 (1) time(s) more—96 (36) stitches total.

Next Round Slip stitch around.

Next Round Single crochet around, working through the back loop only. Work even in single crochet for 5 (1) rounds.

Next Round Slip stitch around.

Fasten off.

FINISHING

Weave in ends. Secure end of beginning chain to inside of hat to form a loop. Block the hat lightly by dampening and stretching it over a plate of similar circumference.

3.

SIMPLE HATS
WITH A TWIST

Using only basic stitches, the designs in this chapter incorporate design details and fun finishes that will add flair to your finished product. But don't be intimidated, these projects just look complex. The colorwork and techniques called for are as simple as striping and basic embroidery.

BABKA HAT

DESIGNED BY LIDIA KARABINECH

CROCHET/INTERMEDIATE

Bobbles add the right amount of interest to this hat.

SIZE

S/M (M/L)

20" (22") [51 (56) cm] circumference x 7" (7½") [18 (19) cm] depth

MATERIALS

 LION BRAND WOOL-EASE
80% ACRYLIC, 20% WOOL
3 OZ (85 G) 197 YD (180 M) BALL

1 ball each #179 Chestnut Heather (MC), #153 Black (CC), or colors of your choice

• Size G-6 (4 mm) crochet hook *or size to obtain gauge*

GAUGE

17 stitches + 20 rounds = 4" (10 cm) over single crochet.
Be sure to check your gauge.

NOTE

• The hat is worked in rounds. Join each round by working a slip stitch in the first stitch of the round.

STITCH EXPLANATION

Bobble Work 5 single crochet in 1 stitch. Drop the loop from the hook, then insert the hook into the first stitch made, then draw the dropped loop through.

Single crochet 2 together (single crochet decrease) Insert the hook into the stitch and draw up a loop. Insert the hook into the next stitch and draw up a loop. Yarn over, draw through all 3 loops on hook (see page 11).

HAT

With MC, chain 4. Join with slip stitch in the first chain to form a ring.

Round 1 Chain 1, work 6 single crochet into the ring.

Round 2 Chain 1, work 2 single crochet in each stitch—12 stitches total.

Round 3 Chain 1, *single crochet in the next stitch, work 2 single crochet in the next stitch; repeat from * around—18 stitches total.

Round 4 Chain 1, *single crochet in the next 2 stitches, work 2 single crochet in the next stitch; repeat from * around—24 stitches total.

Round 5 Chain 1, *single crochet in the next 3 stitches, work 2 single crochet in the next stitch; repeat from * around—30 stitches total.

Round 6 Chain 1, *single crochet in the next 4 stitches, work 2 single crochet in the next stitch; repeat from * around—36 stitches total.

Round 7 Chain 1, *single crochet in the next stitch, make bobble in the next stitch; repeat from * around. Join round with a slip stitch in the first stitch.

Round 8 Chain 1, *single crochet in the next 5 stitches, work 2 single crochet in the next stitch; repeat from * around—42 stitches total.

Round 9 Chain 1, *single crochet in the next 6 stitches, work 2 single crochet in the next stitch; repeat from * around—48 stitches total.

Round 10 Chain 1, *single crochet in the next 7 stitches, work 2 single crochet in the next stitch; repeat from * around—54 stitches total. Join round with a slip stitch in the first stitch.

Round 11 Chain 1, *single crochet in the next 8 stitches, work 2 single crochet in the next stitch; repeat from * around—60 stitches total. Join round with a slip stitch in the first stitch.

Round 12 Chain 1, *single crochet in the next 9 stitches, work 2 single crochet in the next stitch; repeat from * around—66 stitches total. Join round with a slip stitch in the first stitch.

Round 13 Chain 1, *single crochet in next stitch, make bobble in the next stitch; repeat from * around.

Round 14 Chain 1, *single crochet in the next 10 stitches, work 2 single crochet in the next stitch; repeat from * around—72 stitches total.

Round 15 Chain 1, *single crochet in the next 17 (11) stitches, work 2 single crochet in the next stitch; repeat from * around—76 (78) stitches total.

Round 16 Chain 1, *single crochet in the next 18 (12) stitches, work 2 single crochet in the next stitch; repeat from * around—80 (84) stitches total.

Round 17 Chain 1, *single crochet in the next 19 (13) stitches, work 2 single crochet in the next stitch; repeat from * around—84 (90) stitches total.

Round 18 Chain 1, *single crochet in the next 20 (14) stitches, work 2 single crochet in the next stitch; repeat from * around—88 (96) stitches total.

Round 19 Chain 1, *single crochet in the next 21 (15) stitches, work 2 single crochet in the next stitch; repeat from * around—92 (102) stitches total.

Round 20 Chain 1, *single crochet in the next 22 (16) stitches, work 2 single crochet in the next stitch; repeat from * around—96 (108) stitches total.

Rounds 21–25 Chain 1, single crochet in each stitch around.

Round 26 Chain 1, *single crochet 2 together, single crochet in the next 22 (16) stitches; repeat from * around—92 (102) stitches total.

Rounds 27–31 Chain 1, single crochet in each stitch around.

Round 32 Chain 1, *single crochet 2 together, single crochet in the next 21 (15) stitches; repeat from * around—88 (96) stitches total.

Rounds 33–38 Repeat Round 27. Fasten off.

BOTTOM EDGING

Round 1 Join CC with a slip stitch in the last slip stitch made. Repeat Round 27.

Round 2 Chain 1—counts as 1 single crochet, chain 3, double crochet in the same stitch as joining, single crochet in the next 2 stitches, *work (single crochet, chain 3, double crochet) in the next stitch, single crochet in the next 2 stitches; repeat from * around. Fasten off.

FINISHING

BOBBLE TRIM

Position hat so the crown is at the top. Count 6 rounds down from the last round of bobbles (Round 13). Working from front to back to front around the joining stitch of the 6th round, join MC with a slip stitch.

BOBBLE ROUND

Chain 1, *single crochet around next stitch, bobble around next stitch; repeat from * around. Fasten off. Count 5 MC rounds up from the bottom edge. Working from front to back to front around joining stitch of 5th round, join CC with a slip stitch. Work bobble round. Fasten off. Weave in ends.

HAPPY TRAILS

DESIGNED BY REBECCA ROSEN

KNIT/EASY

You won't believe how easy it is to knit this chic hat. First knit the earflaps, then knit across the row for a simple back-and-forth project.

SIZES

S/M (M/L)

20" (21½") [51 (54.5) cm] circumference x 11" (28 cm) depth from base of earflap to crown

MATERIALS

LION BRAND LANDSCAPES
50% WOOL, 50% ACRYLIC
1¾ OZ (50 G) 55 YD (50 M) BALL

2 balls #275 Autumn Trails or color of your choice

- Size 10 (6 mm) knitting needles *or size to obtain gauge*

- Size K-10.5 (6.5 mm) crochet hook

- Two stitch holders

- Large-eyed, blunt needle

- 5" x 5" (12.5 x 12.5 cm) piece of cardboard for tassel

GAUGE

12.5 stitches + 16 rows = 4" (10 cm) over stockinette stitch (knit on right side, purl on wrong side). *Be sure to check your gauge.*

STITCH EXPLANATION

Make 1 An increase worked by moving the left needle from front to back to pick up the horizontal thread of the previous row, lying between needles. Work this new stitch by knitting through the back loop to prevent a hole (see page 91).

EAR FLAPS

Cast on 3 stitches. Knit 1 row.
Increase Row 1 (Wrong Side) Purl 2, make 1, purl 1—4 stitches total.
Knit next row.
Increase Row 2 (Wrong Side) Purl 1, make 1, purl to last stitch, make 1, purl 1—6 stitches total.
Knit next row.
Repeat last 2 rows twice more—10 stitches total.
Work even for 2 rows, then repeat.
Increase Row 2 once more—12 stitches total.

Work even in stockinette stitch until piece measures approximately 3¾" (9.5 cm) from beginning, ending with a right side row. Place stitches on a holder. Make one more earflap, ending with a right side row. Place stitches on holder.

HAT

Next Row (Wrong Side) Cast on 10 (11) stitches onto the right needle, place 12 stitches of the first earflap onto the left needle, then purl across these 12 stitches—22 (23) stitches total on right needle. Cast on 19 (21) stitches onto the right needle—41 (44) stitches total on right needle. Place 12 stitches of the second earflap onto the left needle, then purl across these 12 stitches—53 (56) stitches total on right needle. Cast 10 (11) stitches onto right needle—63 (67) stitches total on right needle.
Next Row (Right Side) Knit 1 (0),

purl 1(0), *knit 2, purl 1; repeat from *, end knit 1.
Next Row Purl 1, *knit 1, purl 2; repeat from *, end
knit 1 (0), purl 1 (0).
Repeat the last 2 rows once more. Work in stockinette stitch
until piece measures 4" (4¼") [10 (11) cm] from the beginning of rib, ending with a wrong side row.

CROWN SHAPING
Decrease Row 1 (Right Side) Knit 3, *knit 2 together, knit 2;
repeat from * across—48 (51) stitches total.
Work 3 rows even.
Decrease Row 2 Knit 2, *knit 2 together, knit 1; repeat from *,
ending knit 1—33 (35) stitches total.
Work 3 rows even.
Decrease Row 3 Knit 3, *knit 2 together; repeat from *, ending
knit 2—19 (20) stitches total.
Purl next row.
Decrease Row 4 Knit 2, *knit 2 together; repeat from *, ending
knit 1 (2)—11 (12) stitches total. Cut yarn, leaving a long tail
for sewing. Thread tail into large-eyed, blunt needle and
weave through remaining stitches. Pull tight to gather
stitches and close the top of hat, fasten securely, then sew
back seam.

FINISHING
EDGING
With crochet hook and right side facing, join yarn with a slip
stitch in the back seam.
Round 1 Chain 1, making sure that work lies flat, single crochet evenly around the entire edge. Join round with a slip
stitch in the first single crochet. Fasten off.
Make two tassels following directions on page 14. Sew one
tassel at the bottom of each earflap.

HAPPY TRAILS

JUST RIBBING

DESIGNED BY
REBECCA ROSEN

KNIT/EASY

There's a reason watchcaps are so popular—every guy looks great in them. Wear it straight or fold up the brim for added warmth. This version, in a smooth wool-blend yarn, is sure to be a favorite.

SIZE

S/M (M/L)
19" (20½") [48.5 (52) cm circumference x 7½" (8") [19 (20.5) cm] depth

MATERIALS

 LION BRAND KOOL WOOL
50% MERINO WOOL,
50% ACRYLIC
1¾ OZ (50 G) 60 YD (54 M) BALL

1 ball #123 Camel Heather or color of your choice

- Size 10.5 (6.5 mm) double-pointed needles—set of four
  or size to obtain gauge

- Stitch marker

- Large-eyed, blunt needle

GAUGE

15 stitches + 17 rows = 4" (10 cm) over rib pattern. *Be sure to check your gauge.*

HAT

Cast on 66 (72) stitches. Divide stitches evenly between 3 needles. Join and place marker to mark beginning of rounds. Work in knit 3, purl 3 rib until piece measures 6½" (16.5 cm) from beginning.

CROWN SHAPING

Decrease Round 1 [Knit 2 together, knit 1, purl 3, knit 3, purl 3] 5 (6) times, ending knit 2 (0) together, knit 1 (0), purl 3 (0)—60 (66) stitches total.

Next 2 Rounds Knit the knit stitches and purl the purl stitches.

Decrease Round 2 [Knit 2, purl 3, knit 2 together, knit 1, purl 3] 5 (6) times, ending knit 2 (0), purl 3 (0)—55 (60) stitches total.

Next 2 Rounds Knit the knit stitches and purl the purl stitches.

Decrease Round 3 [Knit 2, purl 2 together, purl 1, knit 2, purl 3] 5 (6) times, ending knit 2 (0), purl 2 (0) together, purl 1 (0)—49 (54) stitches total.

Next Round Knit the knit stitches and purl the purl stitches.

Decrease Round 4 [Knit 2, purl 2, knit 2, purl 2 together, purl 1] 5 (6) times, ending knit 2 (0), purl 2 (0)—44 (48) stitches total.

Next Round Knit the knit stitches and purl the purl stitches.

Decrease Round 5 [Knit 2 together, purl 2, knit 2, purl 2] 5 (6) times, ending knit 2 (0) together, purl 2 (0)—38 (42) stitches total.

Decrease Round 6 [Knit 1, purl 2, knit 2 together, purl 2] 5 (6) times, ending knit 1 (0), purl 2 (0)—33 (36) stitches total.

Decrease Round 7 [Knit 1, purl 2 together, knit 1, purl 2] 5 (6) times, ending knit 1 (0), purl 2 (0) together—27 (32) stitches total.

Decrease Round 8 [Knit 1, purl 1, knit 1, purl 2 together] 5 (6) times, ending knit 1 (0), purl 1 (0)—22 (26) stitches total.

Decrease Round 9 Knit 1 (0), [knit 2 together] 10 (13) times, then knit the last purl stitch together with the first knit stitch—11 (13) stitches total.

FINISHING

Cut yarn leaving a long tail. Thread tail into large-eyed, blunt needle and weave through remaining stitches. Pull tight to gather; fasten off securely. Weave in ends.

CAROUSEL HAT

DESIGNED BY TRACI BUNKERS

KNIT/EASY

Garter stitch stripes in a fresh, funky color combination are trimmed with an easy-to-crochet bobbled edge for a fun hat you'll be wearing in no time.

SIZE

S (M, L)

20" (21", 22") [51 (53.5, 56) cm] circumference x 7½" (7¾", 8") [19 (19.5, 20.5) cm] depth

MATERIALS

LION BRAND WOOL-EASE 80% ACRYLIC, 20% WOOL 3 OZ (85 G) 197 YD (180 M) BALL

1 ball each #177 Loden (A), #171 Gold (B), #137 Fuchsia (C), #179 Chestnut Heather (D), or colors of your choice

- Size 8 (5 mm) knitting needles *or size to obtain gauge*
- Size H-8 (5 mm) crochet hook for trim
- Large-eyed, blunt needle

GAUGE

18 stitches + 36 rows = 4" (10 cm) over garter stitch (knit every row). *Be sure to check your gauge.*

NOTES

- When working Stripe Pattern 1, carry colors up along the side edge until the last stripe is completed, then cut all but color A.

- When working Stripe Pattern 2, carry color up along the side edge until the last stripe of that color is completed, then cut color.

- Join new colors as needed.

HAT

With A, cast on 85 (89, 93) stitches.

BRIM

Knit 1 row and mark as wrong side. Continue in garter stitch and

Stripe Pattern 1 as follows: *Work 2 rows each using B, C, D, and A; repeat from * once more. Cut all colors except A.

BODY

Knit 5 (7, 9) more rows using A. **Note** What was the wrong side of the brim is now the right side of body. Continue in garter stitch and work **Stripe Pattern 2** as follows: 2 rows B, 2 rows A, 6 rows B, 2 rows C, 2 rows B, 6 rows C, 2 rows D, 2 rows C, 6 rows D, 2 rows A, 2 rows D and 6 rows A.

CROWN SHAPING

Repeat start of Stripe Pattern 2 and, AT SAME TIME, shape crown as follows:

Row 1 (Right Side) *Knit 19 (20, 21), knit 2 together; repeat from *, ending knit 1—81 (85, 89) stitches total.

Row 2 and all Wrong Side Rows Knit.

Row 3 *Knit 18 (19, 20), knit 2 together; repeat from *, ending knit 1—77 (81, 85) stitches total.

Row 5 *Knit 17 (18, 19), knit 2 together; repeat from *, ending knit 1—73 (77, 81) stitches total.

Row 7 *Knit 16 (17, 18), knit 2 together; repeat from *, ending knit 1—69 (73, 77) stitches total.

Row 9 *Knit 15 (16, 17), knit 2 together; repeat from *, ending knit 1—65 (69, 73) stitches total.

Row 11 *Knit 14 (15, 16), knit 2 together; repeat from *, ending knit 1—61 (65, 69) stitches total.

Row 13 *Knit 13 (14, 15), knit 2 together; repeat from *, ending knit 1—57 (61, 65) stitches total.

Row 15 *Knit 5 (4, 6), knit 2 together; repeat from *, ending knit 1—49 (51, 57) stitches total.

Row 17 *Knit 4 (5, 5), knit 2 together; repeat from *, ending knit 1—41 (41, 49) stitches total.

Row 19 *Knit 3 (3, 4), knit 2 together; repeat from *, ending knit 1—33 (33, 41) stitches total.

Row 21 *Knit 2 (2, 3), knit 2 together; repeat from *, ending knit 1—25 (25, 33) stitches total.

Row 23 *Knit 1 (1, 2), knit 2 together; repeat from *, ending knit 1—17 (17, 25) stitches total.

Row 25 FOR SIZE LARGE ONLY *Knit 1, knit 2 together; repeat from *, ending knit 1—17 stitches total.

Rows 25 (25, 27) [Knit 2 together] 8 times, knit 1—9 stitches total. Cut yarn leaving a long tail for sewing. Thread tail into large-eyed, blunt needle and weave through remaining stitches. Pull tight to gather, fasten securely. Sew back seam, reversing seam for brim so seam falls to wrong side.

FINISHING

Position hat so the right side of brim is facing and the cast-on edge is at the top. With crochet hook, join A with a slip stitch in the back seam, *chain 4 for trim, work 4 half double crochet in the 2nd chain from hook, slip stitch in the next 2 chain, then slip stitch in the same stitch as the slip stitch at the base of trim, slip stitch in the next 3 stitches of the cast-on edge; repeat from * around. Join round with a slip stitch in the first slip stitch. Fasten off. Weave in ends.

CAROUSEL HAT

VINTAGE VINES

DESIGNED BY LIDIA KARABINECH

KNIT/INTERMEDIATE

Knit this simple, close-fitting cap and embellish it with separately crocheted flowers and easy-to-do chain stitch embroidery.

SIZE

S (M, L)

18" (19½", 21") [45.5 (49.5, 53.5) cm] circumference x 7" (7½", 8") [18 (19, 20.5) cm] depth

MATERIALS

 LION BRAND WOOL-EASE 80% ACRYLIC, 20% WOOL 3 OZ (85 G) 197 YD (180 M) BALL

2 balls #152 Oxford Grey (A), 1 ball #139 Dark Rose Heather (B), 1 ball #140 Rose Heather (C), 1 ball #130 Green Heather (D), or colors of your choices

- Size 8 (5 mm) 16" (40.5 cm) circular needle *or size to obtain gauge*

- Size 8 (5 mm) double-pointed needles—set of four

- Size J-10 (6 mm) crochet hook for flower

- Stitch marker

- Large-eyed, blunt needle

GAUGE

20 stitches + 18 rounds = 4" (10 cm) over Twisted Rib pattern using 2 strands of A held together. *Be sure to check your gauge.*

PATTERN STITCH

TWISTED RIB (OVER AN EVEN NUMBER OF STITCHES)

Round 1 *Knit 1 through the back loop, purl 1; repeat from * around. Repeat Round 1 for Twisted Rib pattern.

NOTE

- Use 2 strands of A held together throughout.

HAT

With circular needle and 2 strands of A held together, cast on 90 (98, 106) stitches. Join, being careful not to twist, and place marker to mark beginning of round. Work in Twisted Rib pattern until piece measures 6½" (7", 7½") [16.5 (18, 19 cm] from beginning.

CROWN SHAPING

Note Change to double-pointed needles when necessary.

Decrease Round 1 *Knit 1 through the back loop, knit 2 together through the back loop, purl 1; repeat from * around, ending knit 1 through the back loop, purl 1— 68 (74, 80) stitches total.

Next Round Knit the knit stitches through back loops, purl the purl stitches.

Decrease Round 2 Knit 2 through the back loop, *knit 2 together through the back loops, knit 1 through the back loop; repeat from * around—46 (50, 54) stitches total. Knit next round through the back loops.

Decrease Round 3 Knit 0 (2, 0) together through the back loop, *knit 1 through the back loop, knit 2 together through the back loops;

repeat from ✳ around, end knit 1
(0, 0) through back loop—31 (33,
36) stitches total.
Knit next round through the back
loops.

Decrease Round 4 [Knit 2 together
through the back loops] 15 (16, 18)
times, end knit 1 (1, 0) through the
back loop—16 (17, 18) stitches total.

Decrease Round 5 [Knit 2 together
through the back loops] 8 times, end
knit 0 (1, 0)—8 (9, 9) stitches total.
Cut yarn leaving a 10" (25.5 cm)
tail. Thread tail into large-eyed,
blunt needle and weave yarn
through remaining stitches. Pull
tight to gather, then fasten off
securely.

FINISHING

Make one crocheted flower with B
and one with C, following directions on page 15. Sew flower onto
hat. With 2 strands of D, embroi-
der chain-stitch stems and tendrils
as shown, or as desired.

VINTAGE VINES

4.

GRANNY SQUARES

As simple geometric shapes, granny squares are perfect building blocks for hats. Using single or multiple colors, granny squares are portable projects, allowing you to satisfy your stitching needs anywhere.

MAKING A GRANNY SQUARE

Forming a ring is the first step. Chain as many stitches as the pattern dictates, insert the hook into the first chain above the slip knot (illustration 1), yarn over the hook and pull through the first chain and the chain on the hook (illustration 2).

Working into the ring (or under the chain): After you have created the ring, chain 3 chains if you are using double crochet, yarn over and insert the hook under the ring, yarn over and pull up a stitch. When you are working your third or larger rounds, make sure you insert your hook completely underneath the chain below it (illustration 3).

A handy tip when you begin each round is to hold the tail yarn on top of the chain you are crocheting into and crochet the tail so that it is tucked into the chain. This secures the tails as you work, making it easier to weave them later. It is a good idea to weave in the yarn tails as you go so you won't be faced with dozens of ends to weave when you have finished your project and are anxious to show it off.

For seaming information, see page 19.

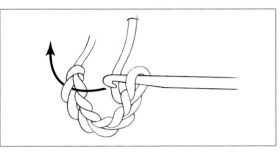

1. Joining granny square ring: insert hook into first chain stitch.

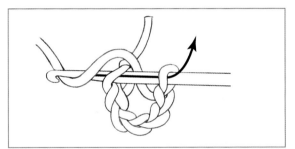

2. Yarn over, pull through chain and stitch on hook.

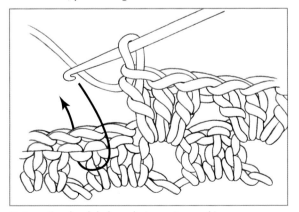

3. Inserting hook below chain you're working on.

PURPLE PILLBOX

DESIGNED BY TRACI BUNKERS

CROCHET/EASY

The simple construction of this granny topper produces over-the-top results. Just crochet five squares and sew them together. A great project for using leftover yarns.

SIZE

21" (53.5 cm) circumference x 8" (20.5 cm) depth

MATERIALS

5 BULKY LION BRAND KOOL WOOL 50% MERINO WOOL, 50% ACRYLIC 1³/₄ OZ (50 G) 60 YD (54 M) BALL

1 ball #130 Grass (A), 2 balls #147 Eggplant (B), 1 ball #114 Denim (C), or colors of your choice

• Size K-10.5 (6.5 mm) crochet hook *or size to obtain gauge*

• Large-eyed, blunt needle

GAUGE

One square = 5" (12.5 cm). *Be sure to check your gauge.*

STITCH EXPLANATION

Bullion Wrap the yarn around the hook 5 times, insert the hook into the chain and draw up a loop, yarn over, draw through all loops on hook, chain 1.

GRANNY SQUARE—MAKE 5

Round 1 With A, chain 3, work 1 bullion in the 3rd chain from the hook, chain 1 more for corner, [make 2 more bullions in the same chain, chain 1 more for corner] 3 times, make 1 bullion in the same chain, slip stitch to top of the beginning chain-3—8 bullions and 4 chain-2 corner spaces total. Fasten off.

Round 2 Join B with a slip stitch in any corner chain-2 space, chain 1, work (2 single crochet, chain 2, 2 single crochet) in the same corner space, *work 2 single crochet between the next 2 bullions, in the next corner space work (2 single crochet, chain 2, 2 single crochet); repeat from * twice more, work 2 single crochet between the next 2 bullions, join round with a slip stitch in the top of the beginning chain-1—24 single crochet total. Fasten off.

Round 3 Join C with a slip stitch in any corner chain-2 space, chain 3 (counts as 1 single crochet and chain 2), single crochet in the same corner space, *single crochet in each of the next 6 single crochet, work (single crochet, chain 2, single crochet) in the corner space; repeat from * twice more, single crochet in each of the next 6 single crochet, join round with a slip stitch in the first chain—32 single crochet total. Fasten off.

Round 4 Join B with a slip stitch in the back loop of a 2nd chain in any corner chain-2 space, chain 2 (counts as 1 half double crochet), work half double crochet in back loop of each of the next 9 stitches, chain 2 for corner, * half double crochet in back loop of the next 10 stitches, chain 2; repeat from * twice more, join round with a slip stitch in the top of the beginning chain-2—40 half double crochet total. Fasten off.

FINISHING

Mark each corner chain-2 space as follows: thread a large-eyed, blunt needle with a 6" (15 cm) strand of contrasting color yarn. From right side of work, insert needle into the first chain, then bring needle up through the 2nd chain. Remove needle, allowing strands to remain.

ASSEMBLY

Hold 2 squares together, wrong side facing. Working through the back loops only of both squares, join A with a slip stitch inside marked stitches, chain 1. Working from left to right, work reverse single crochet in the back loops across to next marked stitch—12 stitches total. Fasten off, leaving corner markers intact. Working in the same manner, join the next 2 squares together forming a ring for the sides of hat. Join the last square to the top, matching the markers at the corners and also going through end of the reverse single crochet joining row with 2nd corner stitches—12 reverse single crochet per side total. Join round with a slip stitch in beginning chain-1. Fasten off. Remove CC yarn markers from corners now.

EDGING

Carefully join A with a slip stitch in any stitch along the bottom edge.

Round 1 Chain 1 (always counts as 1 single crochet), single crochet in the back loop of each stitch and in the end of the reverse single crochet joining row—52 single crochet total. Join the round with a slip stitch in the beginning chain-1. Fasten off.

Round 2 Working through both loops, join B with a slip stitch in any stitch, chain 1, single crochet in each single crochet around. Join round with a slip stitch to beginning chain-1. Fasten off.

Round 3 Working through both loops, join C with a slip stitch in any stitch, chain 1, work reverse single crochet in each stitch around. Join with a slip stitch in beginning chain-1. Fasten off. Weave in ends.

FLAPPER GRANNY

DESIGNED BY LINDA CYR

CROCHET/INTERMEDIATE

Squares become diamonds when you rotate your granny 45 degrees for this funky earflap hat.

SIZE
22³/₄" (58 cm) circumference x 8" (20.5 cm) depth without earflaps

MATERIALS

4 MEDIUM LION BRAND COTTON-EASE 50% COTTON, 50% ACRYLIC 3¹/₂ OZ (100 G) 207 YD (189 M) BALL

1 ball each #153 Licorice (A), #144 Sugarplum (B), #156 Mint (C), #107 Candy Blue (D), or colors of your choice

• Size G-6 (4 mm) crochet hook *or size to obtain gauge*

• Small safety pin

• Large-eyed, blunt needle

GAUGE
16 stitches + 18 rounds = 4" (10 cm) over single crochet.
One granny square = 4¹/₂" (11.5 cm).
Be sure to check your gauge.

NOTE
• Hat is worked in a spiral. Mark the last stitch made in each round with the safety pin to indicate the end of round.

HAT
Beginning at the top edge, with A, chain 91. Taking care not to twist the chain, join with slip stitch in the first chain to form a ring. Working in single crochet, work in stripe pattern as follows: 12 rounds A, 1 round B, 1 round C, 1 round D, and 18 rounds A.
Last Round With A, slip stitch in each stitch around. Fasten off.

GRANNY SQUARE EARFLAPS
With B, chain 4. Join chain with a slip stitch to form a ring.
Round 1 (Right Side) Chain 3 (always counts as 1 double crochet), work 2 double crochet over ring, chain 2, *work 3 double crochet over ring, chain 2; repeat from * 2 more times. Join round with a slip stitch in the 3rd chain of chain-3. Fasten off. From right side, join C with a slip stitch in any chain-2 space.
Round 2 Chain 3, work 2 double crochet in the same chain-2 space, chain 1, *work (3 double crochet, chain 2, 3 double crochet) in next chain-2 space, chain 1; repeat from * 2 more times, ending with 3 double crochet in the beginning chain-2 space, chain 2. Join round with a slip stitch in 3rd chain of chain-3. Fasten off. From right side, join D with a slip stitch in any chain-2 space.
Round 3 Chain 3, work 2 double crochet in the same chain-2 space, chain 1, * work 3 double crochet in the next chain-1 space, chain 1, work (3 double crochet, chain 2, 3 double crochet) in the next chain-2 space, chain 1, repeat from * 2

more times, ending with 3 double crochet in the next chain-1 space, chain 1, 3 double crochet in beginning chain-2 space, chain 2. Join round with a slip stitch in the 3rd chain of chain-3. Fasten off. From right side, join B with a slip stitch in any chain-2 space.

Round 4 Chain 3, work 2 double crochet in the same chain-2 space, chain 1, * [work 3 double crochet in next chain-1 space, chain 1] twice, work (3 double crochet, chain 2, 3 double crochet) in the next chain-2 space, chain 1, repeat from * 2 more times, ending with [work 3 double crochet in next chain-1 space, chain 1] twice, 3 double crochet in the beginning chain-2 space, chain 2. Join round with a slip stitch in 3rd chain of chain-3. Fasten off. From right side, join A with a slip stitch in any chain-2 space.

Round 5 Chain 1 (counts as 1 single crochet), then single crochet in each stitch around, working 3 single crochet in each corner chain-2 space. Join round with a slip stitch in the first single crochet. Fasten off. Weave in ends.

FINISHING

Fold hat in half. Place a piece of contrasting color yarn to serve as a marker at each fold. Fold in the opposite direction, matching yarn markers at center. Place a yarn marker at each fold. Bring all yarn markers together so they meet at the center; the top of hat will form a "+". Whipstitch edges together, forming four points. Bring points together, then tack in place. Try on hat to determine position of earflaps. Place earflaps, on the diagonal, to cover ears. Remove hat, sew earflaps in place.

TASSELS

For top of hat, cut four 18" (46 cm) strands each of B, C and D. Draw strands through top of the hat, so they are doubled. Group colors together, then braid for 5" (12.5 cm). Tie ends with an overhand knot close to braid. Trim ends even for tassel. For each earflap, cut four 18" (46 cm) strands each of B, C and D. Draw strands through chain-2 space at the bottom corner. Continue to work as for top of hat.

SUNNY SIDE UP

DESIGNED BY LINDA CYR

CROCHET/INTERMEDIATE

Keep the sun off your nose with this cheerful hat. Crocheted in cool cotton, it's perfect for warm weather. Granny square motifs let in the cool summer breezes.

SIZE
22½" (57 cm) circumference x 6½" (17 cm) depth without brim

MATERIALS

 LION BRAND LION COTTON 100% COTTON 5 OZ (140 G) 236 YD (216 M) BALL

- 1 ball #157 Sunflower or color of your choice

- Size G-6 (4 mm) crochet hook *or size to obtain gauge*

- Small safety pin

GAUGE
16 stitches + 17 rounds = 4" (10 cm) over single crochet.
One flower motif = 2½" (6.5 cm).
Be sure to check your gauge.

STITCH EXPLANATIONS
Single crochet 2 together (single crochet decrease) Insert hook into stitch and draw up a loop. Insert hook into the next stitch and draw up a loop. Yarn over, draw through all 3 loops on hook (see page 11).
Single crochet 3 together Insert hook into stitch and draw up a loop. [Insert hook into the next stitch and draw up a loop] twice. Yarn over, draw through all 4 loops on hook.
Cluster stitch [Yarn over, draw up a loop, yarn over and draw through 2 loops on hook] 3 times in ring, yarn over and draw through all 4 loops on hook.

HATBAND
FLOWER MOTIF 1
Chain 6. Join chain with a slip stitch in the first chain to form a ring.
Round 1 Chain 3 (counts as 1 double crochet), [work yarn over, draw up a loop, yarn over and draw through 2 loops on hook] twice in ring, yarn over and draw through all 3 loops on hook, [chain 3, cluster stitch in ring] 7 times, chain 3. Join round with a slip stitch in the 3rd chain of beginning chain-3.
Round 2 Slip stitch to center of next chain-3 space, chain 1, single crochet in the same space, [chain 3, single crochet in the next chain-3 space, chain 5, single crochet in the next chain-3 space] 3 times, chain 3, single crochet in the next chain-3 space, chain 2. Join round with a double crochet in the first single crochet—counts as last chain-5 space. Fasten off.

FLOWER MOTIF 2
Work Round 1 as for Motif 1.

JOINING
Round 2 Slip stitch to center of next

chain-3 space, chain 1, single crochet in the same space, chain 3, single crochet in the next chain-3 space, chain 2. With wrong side facing, hold Motif 1 behind Motif 2. Single crochet in chain-5 space of Motif 1, chain 2, single crochet in the next chain-3 space of Motif 2, chain 1, single crochet in the next chain-3 space of Motif 1, chain 1, single crochet in the next chain-3 space of Motif 2, chain 2, single crochet in the next chain-5 space of Motif 1, chain 2, single crochet in the next chain-3 space of Motif 2. Working Motif 2 only, chain 3, single crochet in the next chain-3 space, chain 5, single crochet in the next chain-3 space, chain 3, single crochet in next chain-3 space, chain 2. Join round of Motif 2 with a double crochet in the first single crochet (counts as last chain-5 space). Fasten off.

FLOWER MOTIFS 3–7
Work each motif same as for Motif 2. When working Round 2 (joining round) the last motif joined is now called Motif 1 and the motif being joined is now called Motif 2.

FLOWER MOTIF 8
Work Round 1 as for Motif 1.

... ... hain 1, sin-
... space of Motif 7, chain

1, single crochet in the next chain-3 space of Motif 8, chain 2, single crochet in the next chain-5 space of Motif 7, chain 2, single crochet in the next chain-3 space of Motif 8, chain 3, single crochet in the next chain-3 space of Motif 8, chain 2. With wrong side facing, hold Motif 1 behind Motif 8. Single crochet in chain-5 space of Motif 1, chain 2, single crochet in the next chain-3 space of Motif 8, chain 1, single crochet in the next chain-3 space of Motif 1, chain 1, single crochet in the next chain-3 space of Motif 8, chain 2, single crochet in the next chain-5 space of Motif 1. Join round of Motif 8 with a double crochet in the first single crochet (counts as last chain-5 space). Fasten off.

HAT
CROWN
From right side, join yarn with a slip stitch in first chain-space of any motif of hatband.

Round 1 Work 10 single crochet into the top of each motif—90 stitches total. Mark the last stitch made with a safety pin. You will be working in a spiral, marking the last stitch made with the safety pin to indicate the end of round.

Round 2 Single crochet in each stitch around.

Round 3 Slip stitch in each stitch around.

Round 4 Working through back loops only, single crochet in each stitch around.

CROWN SHAPING
Round 1 *Single crochet in the next 13 stitches, single crochet 2 together; repeat from * around—84 stitches total.

Round 2 *Single crochet in the next 12 stitches, single

crochet 2 together; repeat from * around—78 stitches total.

Round 3 *Single crochet in the next 11 stitches, single crochet 2 together; repeat from * around—72 stitches total.

Round 4 *Single crochet in the next 10 stitches, single crochet 2 together; repeat from * around—66 stitches total.

Round 5 *Single crochet in the next 9 stitches, single crochet 2 together; repeat from * around—60 stitches total.

Round 6 *Single crochet in the next 8 stitches, single crochet 2 together; repeat from * around—54 stitches total.

Round 7 *Single crochet in the next 7 stitches, single crochet 2 together; repeat from * around—48 stitches total.

Round 8 *Single crochet in the next 6 stitches, single crochet 2 together; repeat from * around—42 stitches total.

Round 9 *Single crochet in the next 5 stitches, single crochet 2 together; repeat from * around—36 stitches total.

Round 10 *Single crochet in the next 4 stitches, single crochet 2 together; repeat from * around—30 stitches total.

Round 11 *Single crochet in the next 3 stitches, single

crochet 2 together; repeat from * around—24 stitches total.

Round 12 *Single crochet in the next 2 stitches, single crochet 2 together; repeat from * around—18 stitches total.

Round 13 *Single crochet in the next stitch, single crochet 2 together; repeat from * around—12 stitches total.

Round 14 * Single crochet 2 together; repeat from * around—6 stitches total.

Round 15 Repeat Round 14—3 stitches total.

Round 16 Single crochet 3 together. Fasten off last stitch.

BRIM
Working on the opposite side of hatband, repeat Rounds 1–4 as for crown. Remove marker.

BRIM SHAPING
Note The increase round is worked in a constant spiral, rather than working separate rounds.
Increase Round [Single crochet in the next 16 stitches, work 2 single crochet in the next stitch] 82 times—172 stitches total. Place marker in last stitch made.
Last Round Slip stitch in each stitch around. Fasten off.

FINISHING
Weave in ends.

5.
CHILDREN'S HATS

These fun hats let kids' personality shine through. Lots of color and interesting shapes make hats they will love to wear. The Kiss (page 64) and Rocky Raccoon (opposite) use simple shaping with a distinctive flair—one has a little tail on top, the other has a long tail on the bottom! On we go to the king's court, where we find the Crown (page 66) and the Jester (page 68), both of which are knit flat and sewn up when you're finished.

ROCKY RACCOON

DESIGNED BY DORIS CHAN

CROCHET/INTERMEDIATE

Your favorite wild child will love this animal-friendly coonskin cap.

SIZE
Child (Adult)
19–20" (21–22") [48.5–51 (53.5–56) cm] circumference x 5" (6") [12.5 (15) cm] depth x 9" (13") [23 (33) cm] tail length

MATERIALS
 LION BRAND FUN FUR
100% POLYESTER
1¾ OZ (50 G) 64 YD (58 M) BALL

1 ball each #126 Chocolate (A), #204 Lava (B), #205 Champagne (C), or colors of your choice

- **Child Size:** Size N-13 (9 mm) crochet hook *or size to obtain gauge*

- **Adult Size:** Size P-15 (10 mm) crochet hook *or size to obtain gauge*

- Small safety pin

- Large-eyed, blunt needle

GAUGE

CHILD SIZE
7 stitches = 4" (10 cm) over single crochet using 2 strands held together and smaller crochet hook.

ADULT SIZE
6 stitches = 4" (10 cm) over single crochet using 2 strands held together and larger crochet hook. *Be sure to check your gauge.*

NOTES

- Use 2 strands of yarn held together throughout.

- When changing colors, draw the new color though 2 loops on the hook to complete single crochet.

- Carry the color not in use loosely from round to round.

- It can be challenging to see the individual stitches when working with furry yarn. For best results, count the stitches as you work each row or round to make sure you do not skip or miss a stitch.

STITCH EXPLANATION
Single crochet 2 together (single crochet decrease) Insert the hook into a stitch and draw up a loop. Insert the hook into the next stitch and draw up a loop. Yarn over, draw through all 3 loops on hook (see page 11).

CAP
With 1 strand each of A and B held together, chain 14.

Row 1 Single crochet in the 2nd chain from the hook and in the next 11 chains, work 3 single crochet in the last chain. Turn to the bottom loops of the foundation chain, then single crochet in each loop across—27 stitches total. Chain 1, turn. **Note** Rounded end of cap is the front and the straight end is the back.

Row 2 Single crochet in the first 12 stitches, [work 2 single crochet in the next stitch] 3 times, single crochet in each stitch to end—30 stitches total. Chain 1, turn.

Row 3 Single crochet in the first 12 stitches, [work 2 single crochet in the next stitch, single crochet in the next stitch] 3 times, single crochet in each stitch to end—33 stitches total. Chain 1, turn.

Rows 4–9 Single crochet in each stitch across. Chain 1, turn EXCEPT after Row 9 is completed, do not turn.

TAIL

Round 1 Work 20 single crochet evenly spaced across the straight back edge. Join work into round with a slip stitch in the first single crochet, keeping right side of work toward inside of the tail tube. Mark the last stitch with a safety pin to mark the end of next round.

Round 2 Chain 1, [single crochet 2 together] 10 times—10 stitches total. Remove safety pin. Fasten off. At the underside of the tail, join 2 strands of C with a slip stitch in the center stitch.

Round 3 Chain 1, single crochet in the same stitch as joining, then single crochet in each stitch around. Mark the last stitch made with safety pin. You will be working in a spiral marking the last stitch made with the safety pin to indicate the end of the round.

Round 4 Single crochet in each single crochet around. Drop C and change to 2 strands of A.

Rounds 5 and 6 Single crochet in each stitch around. When completing Round 6, change to 2 strands of C.

Rounds 7 and 8 Single crochet in each stitch around. When completing Round 8, drop C and change to 2 strands of A.

Repeat Rounds 5–8 for 2 (3) times more; do not change color at the end of the last round. Continue with 2 strands of C to the end.

Next Round With C, [single crochet 2 together] 5 times—5 stitches total.

Last Round Single crochet in each stitch around. Join round with a slip stitch in first stitch.

Cut yarn, leaving a long tail. Thread tail into large-eyed, blunt needle and weave through remaining stitches. Pull tight to gather, then fasten off securely. Weave in ends.

FINISHING

Try on cap to check for fit. If necessary, adjust edging to fit by using a tighter tension (smaller hook) to make smaller, the same tension as before to keep same size, or a looser tension (bigger hook) to make larger.

EDGING

From right side, join 1 strand each of A and B with a slip stitch at the base of the tail.

Round 1 Slip stitch in each stitch around. Join round with a slip stitch. Fasten off. Weave in ends.

THE KISS

DESIGNED BY LINDA CYR

KNIT/EASY

Since the yarn is doubled, this project shapes up twice as quickly.

SIZE

Newborn (Infant, Toddler)
14½" (17", 19") [37 (43, 48.5) cm]
circumference x 5¼" (5¾", 6¾")
[13.5 (14.5, 17) cm] depth

MATERIALS

LION BRAND POLARSPUN
100% POLYESTER
1¾ OZ (50 G) 137 YD (125 M) BALL

1 ball #147 Polar Purple or color of
your choice

- Size 7 and 9 (4.5 and 5.5 mm)
  16" (40.5 cm) circular needles *or
  size to obtain gauge*

- Size 9 (5.5 mm) double-pointed
  needles (dpns)—set of four

- Stitch marker

- Large-eyed, blunt needle

GAUGE

10 stitches + 16 rows = 4" (10 cm)
over stockinette stitch (knit every
round) using 2 strands of yarn held
together and larger needle.
Be sure to check your gauge.

NOTE

- Use 2 strands of yarn held
  together throughout.

HAT

With smaller needle and 2 strands
of yarn held together, cast on 36
(42, 48) stitches. Taking care not to
twist stitches, join and place
marker.
Work in knit 1, purl 1 rib for 1" (2.5
cm). Change to larger needle.
Continue in stockinette stitch and
work even until piece measures
2½" (3", 4") [6.5 (7.5, 10) cm]
from beginning.

CROWN SHAPING

Note Change to double-pointed
needles when necessary.
Decrease Round 1 *Knit 4 (5, 6),
knit 2 together; repeat from *
around—30 (36, 42) stitches total.
Knit next 2 rounds.
Decrease Round 2 *Knit 3 (4, 5),
knit 2 together; repeat from *
around—24 (30, 36) stitches total.
Knit next 2 rounds.
Decrease Round 3 *Knit 2 (3, 4),
knit 2 together; repeat from *
around—18 (24, 30) stitches total.
Knit next 2 rounds.
Decrease Round 4 *Knit 1 (2, 3),
knit 2 together; repeat from *
around—12 (18, 24) stitches total.
Knit next 2 rounds.
For sizes Infant and Toddler only
Decrease Round 5 *Knit 1 (2), knit 2
together; repeat from * around—
12 (18) stitches total.
Knit next round.

For size Toddler only
Decrease Round 6 *Knit 1, knit 2
together; repeat from * around—
12 stitches total.
Knit next round.

For all sizes

Next Decrease Round *Knit 1, knit 2 together; repeat from * around—8 stitches total.

Knit next round.

Last Decrease Round [Knit 2 together] 4 times—4 stitches total. Slide stitches back to the beginning of needle.

BEGIN I-CORD

Next Row (Right Side) With 2nd double-pointed needle,* knit 4, do not turn. Slide stitches back to the beginning to work the next row from the right side; repeat from * until I-cord measures 3½" (9 cm).

FINISHING

Cut yarn leaving a long tail. Thread tail into large-eyed, blunt needle, then weave needle through remaining stitches. Pull tight to gather stitches and fasten off. Insert needle through center of I-cord. Tie I-cord in an overhand knot close to the base of cord. On wrong side, trim off excess tail. Weave in ends.

THE CROWN

DESIGNED BY LISA CARNAHAN

KNIT/INTERMEDIATE

This playful hat is fit for a king or a queen. It's knit back and forth and seamed after you're done.

SIZE
18–24 months (4–6 years)
16" (18") [40.5 (45.5) cm] circumference x 4" (5½") [10 (14) cm] depth

MATERIALS
 LION BRAND COTTON-EASE
50% COTTON, 50% ACRYLIC
3½ OZ (100 G)—207 YD (189 M) BALL

1 ball each #133 Orangeade (A), #169 Pistachio (B), #102 Bubble Gum (C), #158 Pineapple (D), or colors of your choice

• Size 8 (5 mm) 16" circular needle *or size to obtain gauge*

• Size 8 (5 mm) straight knitting needles

• Spare size 8 (5 mm) or smaller needle

• Stitch marker

• Stitch holders

GAUGE
18 stitches + 24 rows = 4" (10 cm) over stockinette stitch (knit on right side, purl on wrong side).
Be sure to check your gauge.

STITCH EXPLANTION

Slip slip knit Slip next 2 stitches as if to knit, one at a time, to right needle; insert left needle into the fronts of these 2 stitches and knit them together (see page 16).

BOTTOM TABS

With straight needles and A, cast on 8 (9) stitches. Knit 5 (7) rows. Cut yarn and place stitches on spare needle. Make 7 more tabs in color order as follows: B, C, D, A, B, C and D. Set aside.

HAT

With circular needle and A, cast on 64 (72) stitches. Join and place marker to mark beginning of rounds. Knit 8 (10) rounds for hatband.

JOINING BOTTOM TABS

Change to B. Hold needle with the bottom tabs in the front of the nee-dle with hatband stitches, then work as follows: *knit 1 stitch from the front needle together with 1 stitch from the back needle; repeat from * around.

Next Round With B, purl, increase 8 (9) stitches evenly spaced around—72 (81) stitches total.

BEGIN STRIPE PATTERN

Rounds 1–5 With C, knit.

Round 6 With D, knit.

Round 7 With D, purl.

Round 8 With A, knit.

Round 9 With A, purl.

Rounds 10–12 With B, knit.

Round 13 With C, knit.

Round 14 With C, purl.

Rounds 15–21 With D, knit.

Round 22 With A, knit.

Round 23 With A, purl.

Round 24 With B, knit.

Round 25 With B, purl.

Round 26 With C, knit.

Round 27 With C, *knit 7, slip slip knit; repeat from * around—64 (72) stitches total.

Round 28 With C, knit.

Round 29 With D, *knit 6, slip slip knit; repeat from * around—56 (63) stitches total.

Round 30 With D, purl. Continue with A only.

Round 31 *Knit 5, slip slip knit; repeat from * around—48 (54) stitches total.

Rounds 32, 34, 36, 38, 40 Knit.

Round 33 *Knit 4, slip slip knit; repeat from * around—40 (45) stitches total.

Round 35 *Knit 3, slip slip knit; repeat from * around—32 (36) stitches total.

Round 37 *Knit 2, slip slip knit; repeat from * around—24 (27) stitches total.

Round 39 *Knit 1, slip slip knit; repeat from * around—16 (18) stitches total.

Round 41 *Knit 2 (7), slip slip knit; repeat from * around—12 (16) stitches total.

TOP TABS

With straight needles and A, knit into the front and back of the next 3 (4) stitches—6 (8) stitches. Place remaining 9 (12) stitches on holder. Working back and forth on these 6 (8) stitches, knit 5 (7) rows. Bind off as if to knit. For next tab, slip the next 3 (4) stitches from holder onto needle. With B, knit into the front and back of each stitch—6 (8) stitches. Knit 5 (7) rows. Bind off as if to knit. Working in the same manner, make 2 more tabs using C and D.

FINISHING

Wrap a strand of B twice around base of top tabs. Pull ends tight to gather top of hat closed. Tie ends securely. Trim excess yarn, then weave in ends.

THE JESTER

DESIGNED BY LISA CARNAHAN

KNIT/INTERMEDIATE

This jester hat is fun to knit and fun to wear. Embellish the ends with your favorite buttons.

SIZE

18–24 months (4–6 years)
16" (18") [40.5 (46.5) cm] circumference x 6" (7") [15 (18 cm] depth

MATERIALS

LION BRAND WATERCOLORS
65% ACRYLIC, 35% MERINO WOOL
1³⁄₄ OZ (50 G) 55 YD (50 M) BALL

1 ball each #339 Sunset Rose (A), #308 Blue Lagoon (B), #347 Purple Haze (C), #373 Pond Green (D), or colors of your choice

- Size 9 (5.5 mm) knitting needles *or size to obtain gauge*

- Size 8 (5 mm) 16" (40.5 cm) circular needle

- Stitch marker

- Large-eyed, blunt needle

- Four 1" (25 mm) buttons

GAUGE

12 stitches + 17 rows = 4" (10 cm) over stockinette stitch (knit on right side, purl on wrong side) using larger needles.
Be sure to check your gauge.

SIDE OF HAT AND UNDERSIDE OF POINT

With straight needles and A, cast on 13 (15) stitches. Work in stockinette stitch for 4¹⁄₂" (5") [11.5 (13) cm], ending with a wrong side row. Mark beginning and end of last row with yarn markers.

SHAPE POINT

Decrease 1 stitch each end on next row, then every 4th row 4 (5) times more, ending with a right side row—3 stitches remain. Work even for 3 rows, ending with a wrong side row.
Next Row (Right Side) Knit 3 together. Fasten off last stitch.

Make 3 more points using colors B, C and D.

TOP OF HAT AND POINT

With straight needles and A, cast on 1 stitch.
Row 1 Knit into the front and back of stitch—2 stitches total.
Row 2 Purl into the front and back of the first stitch, purl 1—3 stitches total.
Row 3 Knit into the front and back of the first stitch, knit to the last stitch, knit into the front and back of the last stitch—5 stitches total.
Row 4 Purl.
Repeat Rows 3 and 4 for 4 (5) times more—13 (15) stitches. Mark the beginning and the end of the last row with stitch markers.

SHAPE POINT

Decrease 1 stitch each end on the next row, then every 4th row 4 (5) times more, ending with a right side row—3 stitches remaining. Work even for 3 rows, ending with a wrong side row.

Next Row (Right Side) Knit 3 together. Fasten off last stitch. Make 3 more points using colors B, C and D.

FINISHING

Sew sides of hat pieces together, matching markers. Sew tops of hat pieces together from cast-on edge to markers. Sew point sections together matching colors.

HATBAND

With wrong side facing, circular needle and A, pick up and knit 48 (56) stitches evenly spaced around the bottom edge of the hat. Join work and place a marker to mark beginning of round.

Round 1 Knit.

Round 2 Purl.

Change to B and repeat Rounds 1 and 2.

For Size 18–24 months only, change to C and repeat Round 1.

For Size 4–6 years, change to C and repeat Rounds 1 and 2.

Change to D and repeat Round 1.

Bind off all stitches as if to purl.

Fold up band. Sew buttons to ends of points. Weave in ends.

THE JESTER

6.

INCORPORATING COLOR

Nothing grabs people's attention faster than color. The hats in this chapter use slip stitch, intarsia, and fair isle techniques to create color patterns in knitting, while stripes in both plain and fancy stitches enliven crochet patterns. Be bold in your color choices and you will never be known as the wallflower.

URBAN CHULLO

DESIGNED BY VLADIMIR TERIOKHIN

CROCHET/INTERMEDIATE

Stripes are the easiest way to incorporate color. Subtle gradations of green and blue make this earflap hat understated enough for him to wear. The picot edging is reminiscent of traditional Chullos worn by men in the Andes.

SIZE

S/M (M/L)

21" (22½") [53.5 (57) cm] circumference x 7½" (8½") [19 (21.5) cm] depth without earflaps

MATERIALS

LION BRAND JIFFY
100% ACRYLIC
SOLID COLORS: 3 OZ (85 G) 135 YD (123 M) BALL

1 ball each #131 Forest Green (A), #109 Royal (B), #173 Grass Green (C), #170 Peacock (D), or colors of your choice

• For size S/M, size J-10 (6 mm) crochet hook *or size to obtain gauge*

• For size M/L, size K-10.5 (6.5 mm) crochet hook *or size to obtain gauge*

GAUGE

13 stitches + 7 rounds = 4" (10 cm) over double crochet using size J-10 (6 mm) hook

12 stitches + 6 rounds = 4" (10 cm) over double crochet using size K-10.5 (6.5 mm) hook

Be sure to check your gauge.

STITCH EXPLANATIONS

Join yarn with a double crochet Make a slip knot and place on hook, then yarn over. Insert the hook into a stitch. Yarn over and draw up a loop. [Yarn over and draw through 2 loops on the hook] twice.

Single crochet 2 together (single crochet decrease) Insert hook into a stitch and draw up a loop. Insert the hook into the next stitch and draw up a loop. Yarn over, draw through all 3 loops on hook (see page 11).

Single crochet 3 together Insert the hook into a stitch and draw up a loop. [Insert the hook into the next stitch and draw up a loop] twice. Yarn over, draw through all 4 loops on hook.

Double crochet 2 together Yarn over, insert the hook into a stitch and draw up a loop, yarn over and draw through 2 loops. Yarn over, insert the hook into the next stitch and draw up a loop. Yarn over, draw through 2 loops, yarn over and draw through all loops on hook.

HAT

With A, chain 6. Join chain with a slip stitch in the first chain to form a ring.

Round 1 Chain 3 (counts as 1 double crochet), work 11 double crochet in ring—12 stitches total. Join the round with a slip stitch in the

3rd chain of beginning chain-3. Fasten off.

Round 2 From right side, join B with a slip stitch in the same stitch as joining, chain 3, work double crochet in the same stitch as joining, [work 2 double crochet in the next stitch] 11 times—24 stitches total. Join the round with a slip stitch in the 3rd chain of beginning chain-3. Fasten off.

Round 3 From right side, join C with a slip stitch in the same stitch as joining, chain 3, work 2 double crochet in the next stitch, *double crochet in the next stitch, work 2 double crochet in the next stitch; repeat from * around—36 stitches total. Join the round with a slip stitch in the 3rd chain of beginning chain-3. Fasten off.

Round 4 From right side, join D with a slip stitch in the same stitch as joining, chain 3, double crochet in the next stitch, work 2 double crochet in the next stitch, *double crochet in the next 2 stitches, work 2 double crochet in the next stitch; repeat from * around—48 stitches total. Join the round with a slip stitch in the 3rd chain of beginning chain-3. Fasten off.

Round 5 From right side, join A with a slip stitch in the same stitch as joining, chain 3, double crochet in each stitch around. Join the round with a slip stitch in the 3rd chain of beginning chain-3. Fasten off.

Round 6 From right side, join B with a slip stitch in the same stitch as joining, chain 3, double crochet in the next 2 stitches, work 2 double crochet in the next stitch, *dou-ble crochet in the next 3 stitches, work 2 double crochet in the next stitch; repeat from * around—60 stitches total. Join the round with a slip stitch in the 3rd chain of beginning chain-3. Fasten off.

Round 7 From right side, join C with a slip stitch in the same stitch as joining, chain 3, double crochet in the next 3 stitches, work 2 double crochet in the next stitch,

*double crochet in the next 6 stitches, work 2 double crochet in the next stitch; repeat from * around, ending double crochet in last 6 stitches—68 stitches total. Join the round with a slip stitch in the 3rd chain of beginning chain-3.

Fasten off.

Round 8 With D, repeat Round 5.

Round 9 With A, repeat Round 5.

Round 10 With B, repeat Round 5.

Round 11 With C, repeat Round 5.

Round 12 With D, repeat Round 5.

Round 13 With A, repeat Round 5.

RIGHT EARFLAP

Position hat so the bottom edge is at the top and the right side of work is facing. Count 8 stitches to the left of the last joining stitch (this is the back of the hat), join B with a double crochet in the next stitch, then double crochet in the next 11 stitches—12 stitches total. Fasten off. Turn.

Row 2 (Wrong Side) Join C with a double crochet in the first stitch, then double crochet in the next 11 stitches. Fasten off. Turn.

Row 3 (Right Side) With D, repeat Row 2. Fasten off. Turn.

Row 4 With A, repeat Row 2. Fasten off. Turn.

Row 5 With B, repeat Row 2. Fasten off. Turn.

Row 6 Join C with a double crochet in the first stitch, double crochet 2 together, double crochet in the next 6 stitches, double crochet 2 together, double crochet in the last stitch—10 stitches total. Fasten off. Turn.

Row 7 Join D with a double crochet in first stitch, double crochet 2 together, double crochet in next 4 stitches, double crochet 2 together, double crochet in last stitch—8 stitches total. Fasten off. Turn.

Row 8 Join A with a double crochet in the first stitch, double crochet 2 together, double crochet in the next 2 stitches, double crochet 2 together, double crochet in the last stitch—6 stitches total. Chain 1, turn.

Row 9 Working in single crochet, [single crochet 2 together] 3 times—3 stitches total. Chain 1, turn.

Row 10 Single crochet 3 together. Fasten off the last stitch securely.

LEFT EARFLAP

Position hat so the bottom edge is at the top and the right side of work is facing. Count 20 stitches to the right of the last joining stitch, join B with a double crochet in the next stitch, then double crochet in the next 11 stitches—12 stitches total. Fasten off. Turn. Repeat Rows 2–10 same as for right earflap.

FINISHING

PICOT EDGING

From right side, join D with a slip stitch in the joining stitch at the back of hat.

Round 1 Making sure that work lies flat, work around entire edge as follows: Chain 1, *single crochet in the next 2 stitches, chain 3, slip stitch in the 3rd chain from the hook; repeat from * around. Join round with a slip stitch in the first single crochet. Fasten off.

MANLY SLIP-STITCH HAT

DESIGNED BY REBECCA ROSEN

KNIT/EASY

Slip stitch knitting, a technique that uses only one color per row, is fun and easy to execute. This hat is knit back and forth and seamed when you're done. Bright contrasting colors and subtle texture complete this chic chapeau.

SIZE
S/M (M/L)
21" (22½") [53.5 (57) cm] circumference x 7½" (8") [19 (20.5) cm] depth

MATERIALS

 LION BRAND KOOL WOOL
50% MERINO WOOL,
50% ACRYLIC
1³/₄ OZ (50 G) 60 YD (54 M) BALL

1 ball each #098 Ivory (A), #130 Grass (B), #153 Black (C),
or colors of your choice

- Size 10.5 (6.5 mm) needles *or size to obtain gauge*

- Large-eyed, blunt needle

GAUGE
13 stitches + 17 rows = 4" (10 cm) over stockinette stitch (knit on right side, purl on wrong side).

Be sure to check your gauge.

STITCH PATTERN
SLIP STITCH PATTERN (MULTIPLE OF 2 STITCHES + 1)
Row 1 (Right Side) Knit 2, *slip 1 with yarn in front, knit 1; repeat from *, ending slip 1 with yarn in front, knit 2.
Row 2 Purl.
Row 3 Knit 3, *slip 1 with yarn in front, knit 1; repeat from *, ending slip 1 with yarn in front, knit 3.
Row 4 Purl.
Repeat Rows 1–4 for Slip Stitch Pattern.

HAT
With A, cast on 69 (73) stitches. Work in knit 1, purl 1 rib for 3 rows, ending with a right side row. Purl next row.
Change to slip stitch pattern and work in color sequence as follows: With B, work Rows 1 and 2; with A, work Rows 3 and 4; with A, work in stockinette stitch for 2 rows. With B, work Rows 1 and 2; with A, work Rows 3 and 4; with C, work Rows 1 and 2; with B, work Rows 3 and 4; with C, work Rows 1 and 2; with C, work in stockinette stitch for 2 rows. With B, work Rows 1 and 2; with C, work Rows 3 and 4; with C, work in stockinette stitch for 2 (4) rows. Continue in stockinette stitch with C only.

CROWN SHAPING
Decrease Row 1 (Right Side) Knit 2, [knit 2 together, knit 2] 16 (17) times, knit 2 together, knit 1—52 (56) stitches total.
Work 3 rows even.
Decrease Row 2 Knit 2, [knit 2 together, knit 1] 16 (18) times, knit

2 (0)—36 (38) stitches total.
Purl next row.

Decrease Row 3 Knit 2, [knit 2
together, knit 1] 11 (12) times, knit
1 (0)—25 (26) stitches total.
Purl next row.

Decrease Row 4 Knit 2, [knit 2
together] 11 (12) times, knit 1 (0)—
14 stitches total.

FINISHING

Cut yarn leaving a long tail for
sewing. Thread tail into large-eyed,
blunt needle and weave through
remaining stitches. Pull tight to
gather, then fasten off securely, and
sew back seam. Weave in ends.

MANLY SLIP-STITCH HAT

CITY SNOWFLAKE

DESIGNED BY LIDIA KARABINECH

KNIT/INTERMEDIATE

The bold black and white snowflake takes this traditional motif off the slopes and into the city.

SIZE

20" (51 cm) circumference x 8½" (21.5 cm) depth

MATERIALS

 LION BRAND KOOL WOOL
50% MERINO WOOL,
50% ACRYLIC
1¾ OZ (50 G) 60 YD (54 M) BALL

2 balls #098 Ivory (MC), 1 ball #153 Black (CC), or colors of your choice

- Size 10.5 (6.5 mm) knitting needles *or size to obtain gauge*

- Large-eyed, blunt needle

- 6" x 6" (15 x 15 cm) piece of cardboard for tassel

GAUGE

12 stitches + 18 rows = 4" (10 cm) over stockinette stitch (knit on right side, purl on wrong side).
Be sure to check your gauge.

NOTES

- When changing colors, pick up the new color from under the dropped color to prevent holes.

- Carry color not in use loosely across the wrong side of work.

INCORPORATING COLOR

STITCH EXPLANATION

Slip knit 2 pass Slip 1 as if to knit, knit 2 together, pass slipped stitch over—2 stitches decreased.

HAT

With MC cast on 61 stitches.

BRIM

Rows 1 and 3 Purl.

Row 2 Knit.

Row 4 Purl. Beginning with a knit row, continue in stockinette stitch.

Begin Chart

Row 1 (Right Side) With MC knit 19, work stitches 1–23 of chart, with MC knit 19. Continue to work in this manner (keeping 19 stitches each side of chart in MC) to Row 23, ending with a right side row.

Next row (Wrong Side) With MC, purl. Continue in stockinette stitch and MC only.

CROWN SHAPING

Row 1 (Right Side) Knit 4, [slip knit 2 pass, knit 7] 5 times, slip knit 2 pass, knit 4—49 stitches total.

Row 2 and all Wrong Side Rows Purl.

Row 3 Knit 3, [slip knit 2 pass, knit 5] 5 times, slip knit 2 pass, knit 3—37 stitches total.

Row 5 Knit 2, [slip knit 2 pass, knit 3] 5 times, slip knit 2 pass, knit 2—25 stitches total.

Row 7 Knit 1, [slip knit 2 pass, knit 1] 5 times, slip knit 2 pass, knit 1—13 stitches total.

Row 9 Knit 2, [slip knit 2 pass, knit 1] twice, slip knit 2 pass—7 stitches. Cut yarn, leaving a long tail for sewing. Thread tail into large-eyed, blunt needle and weave through remaining stitches. Pull tight to gather, fasten off securely, then sew back seam.

FINISHING

TASSEL

Wrap MC and CC 16 times around cardboard. Slip a 20" (51 cm) length of MC and CC under the strands and knot tightly at one end of cardboard. Remove cardboard. Wrap and tie a 10" (25.5 cm) length of MC around the tassel about 1½" (4 cm) down from the top. Cut the loops at the opposite end. Trim ends even. At the top of the tassel, group the color strands together. Knot strands for 1½" (4 cm), alternating left overhand knots and right overhand knots. Sew the tassel to the top of the hat.

DIAMONDS AND LACE

DESIGNED BY VLADIMIR TERIOKHIN

KNIT/INTERMEDIATE

This is a great first project for learning intarsia.

SIZE
18" (45.5 cm) circumference x 8" (20.5 cm) depth

MATERIALS

 LION BRAND JIFFY
100% ACRYLIC
SOLID COLORS: 3 OZ (85 G) 135 YD (123 M) BALL

1 ball each #144 Lilac (A), #124 Camel (B), #158 Lemon (C), or colors of your choice

- Size 10 (6 mm) needles *or size to obtain gauge*

- Large-eyed, blunt needle

GAUGE
14.7 stitches + 18 rows = 4" (10 cm) over stockinette stitch (knit on right side, purl on wrong side). *Be sure to check your gauge.*

STITCH EXPLANATION
Slip knit pass Slip 1, knit 1, pass slipped stitch over knit stitch.

Slip knit 2 pass Slip 1, knit 2 together, pass slipped stitch over— 2 stitches decreased.

NOTES
- Wind each color into 2 separate balls.

- When changing color, pick up the new color from under the dropped color to prevent holes.

HAT
Beginning at the bottom edge, *with A cast on 11 stitches, with B cast on 11 stitches, with C cast on 11 stitches; repeat from * once more—66 stitches.
Keeping in color pattern as established, work in knit 1, purl 1 rib for 1½" (4 cm), ending with a right side row.
Beginning with a purl row, work in stockinette stitch for 3 rows.

BEGIN PATTERN STITCH
Row 1 (Right Side) *Knit 4, knit 2 together, yarn over, knit 5; repeat from * 5 times more.
Row 2 and all Wrong Side rows Purl across each section.
Row 3 *Knit 3, knit 2 together, yarn over, knit 1, yarn over, slip knit pass, knit 3; repeat from * 5 times more.
Row 5 *Knit 2, knit 2 together, yarn over, knit 3, yarn over, slip knit pass, knit 2; repeat from * 5 times more.
Row 7 *Knit 1, knit 2 together, yarn over, knit 5, yarn over, slip knit pass, knit 1; repeat from * 5 times more.
Row 9 *Knit 2, yarn over, slip knit pass, knit 3, knit 2 together, yarn over, knit 2; repeat from * 5 times more.
Row 11 *Knit 3, yarn over, slip knit pass, knit 1, knit 2 together,

yarn over, knit 3; repeat from * 5 times more.

Row 13 *Knit 4, yarn over, slip knit 2 pass, yarn over, knit 4; repeat from * 5 times more.

Row 15 *Knit 4, slip knit pass, yarn over, knit 5; repeat from * 5 times more.

Rows 17 and 19 Knit across each section.

CROWN SHAPING

Row 21 *Slip knit pass, knit 7, knit 2 together; repeat from * 5 times more—54 stitches total.

Row 23 *Slip knit pass, knit 5, knit 2 together; repeat from * 5 times more– 42 stitches total.

Row 25 *Slip knit pass, knit 3, knit 2 together; repeat from * 5 times more—30 stitches total.

Row 27 *Slip knit pass, knit 1, knit 2 together; repeat from * 5 times more—18 stitches total.

Row 29 *Slip knit 2 pass; repeat from * 5 times more—6 stitches total.

FINISHING

Cut yarn from first A section leaving a long tail for sewing; cut remaining yarns leaving a tail long enough to weave in. Thread A tail into a yarn needle and pull through remaining stitches. Pull tight to gather, then sew back seam. Weave in ends.

DIAMONDS AND LACE

PORTICO CAP

DESIGNED BY VLADIMIR TERIOKHIN

CROCHET/INTERMEDIATE

Silver adds a hint of glamour to this shell stitch skullcap. The denim blue color lets you dress it down and wear it with your favorite jeans. Add more flowers for extra impact.

SIZE

Child (Woman)
19" (21") [48.5 (53.5) cm] circumference x 8" (20.5 cm) depth for both sizes
Note Child's size is given first with woman's in parentheses. If there is only one number or step, work for both sizes.

MATERIALS

LION BRAND HOMESPUN (A)
98% ACRYLIC, 2% POLYESTER
6 OZ (170 G) 185 YD (167 M) SKEIN

1 skein #321 Williamsburg or color of your choice

LION BRAND GLITTERSPUN (B)
60% ACRYLIC, 13% POLYESTER,
27% CUPRO
1³/₄ OZ (50 G) 115 YD (105 M) BALL

1 ball #150 Silver or color of your choice

• Size K-10.5 (6.5 mm) crochet hook *or size to obtain gauge*

• Large-eyed, blunt needle

GAUGE

10 single crochet + 16 rows = 4" (10 cm) using A.
Be sure to check your gauge.

NOTE

• Join each round with a slip stitch, changing to new color. Leave unused color on the inside until ready to be used again.

STITCH EXPLANATIONS

V-Stitch (Double crochet, chain 1, double crochet) in the same stitch.
Double V-Stitch (2 double crochet, chain 1, 2 double crochet) in the same stitch.
Triple V-Stitch (3 double crochet, chain 1, 3 double crochet) in the same stitch.

Double crochet 2 together *Yarn over, insert the hook in a stitch and pull up a loop, yarn over, draw through 2 loops; repeat from * once in the next stitch, yarn over, draw through all loops on the hook—1 stitch decreased.

BAND

With A, loosely chain 48 (52). Join with a slip stitch to the first chain. Chain 1, single crochet in the first stitch and each chain around—48 (52) single crochet. Join with a slip stitch, changing to B. *Work 1 round single crochet in B, 1 round single crochet in A; repeat from * once more and fasten off.

BODY

Round 1 With right side facing and working along the other side of the beginning chain, join A with a slip stitch in any chain. Chain 1, single

crochet in the same stitch, *skip 1 chain, triple v-stitch in the next chain, skip 1 chain, single crochet in the next chain; repeat from * around to last 3 stitches; skip 1 chain, triple v-stitch in the next chain, skip 1 chain, join to first single crochet changing to B—12 (13) triple v-stitches.

Round 2 With B, chain 4 (counts as 1 double crochet, chain 1), double crochet in the same stitch, *chain 3, single crochet in chain-1 space of triple v-stitch, chain 3, v-stitch in the next single crochet; repeat from * around to the last triple v-stitch; chain 3, single crochet in the chain-1 space of triple v-stitch, chain 3, join round with A in the 3rd chain of beginning chain-4.

Round 3 With A, slip stitch in chain-1 space, chain 3, (2 double crochet, chain 1, 3 double crochet) in the same space, *single crochet in the next single crochet, triple v-stitch in chain-1 space of v-stitch; repeat from * around ending single crochet in the next single crochet, join in top of beginning chain-3, slip stitch to chain-1 space of triple v-stitch, changing to B.

Round 4 With B, chain 1, single crochet in the same space, *chain 3, v-stitch in the single crochet, chain 3, single crochet in chain-1 space of triple v-stitch; repeat from * around ending with v-stitch in the last single crochet, chain 3, join with A to first single crochet.

Round 5 With A, chain 1, single crochet in same stitch, *triple v-stitch in the next chain-1 space of v-stitch, single crochet in the next single crochet; repeat from * around ending triple v-stitch in v-stitch, join with B to the first single crochet.

Rounds 6–8 Repeat Rounds 2–4.

Round 9 Repeat Round 5, working double v-stitch instead of triple v-stitch.

Round 10 With B, chain 4, double crochet in the same stitch, *chain 2, single crochet in chain-1 space of double v-stitch, chain 2, v-stitch in the next single crochet; repeat from * to last double v-stitch; chain 2, single crochet in chain-1 space of double v-stitch, chain 2, join with A in the 3rd chain of beginning chain-4.

Round 11 With A, slip stitch in chain-1 space, chain 3, 2 double crochet in the same space, continue same as for Round 3 working 3 double crochet instead of triple v-stitch, joining with B to middle of the 3-double crochet group.

Round 12 With B, chain 1, single crochet in the same stitch, *chain 1, v-stitch in the next single crochet, chain 1, single crochet in the middle of 3-double crochet group; repeat from * around ending with a v-stitch in the last single crochet, chain 1, join with A to the first single crochet.

Round 13 Repeat Round 5, working v-stitch instead of triple v-stitch.

Round 14 With B, chain 4, double crochet in the same stitch, *chain 1, single crochet in chain-1 space of v-stitch, chain 1, v-stitch in the next single crochet; repeat from * to last v-stitch; chain 1, single crochet in chain-1 space of v-stitch, chain 1, join with A in the 3rd chain of beginning chain-4.

Round 15 With A, slip stitch in chain-1 space, chain 3 (counts as 1 double crochet), *single crochet in the next single crochet, double crochet in the next chain-1 space of v-stitch; repeat from * around to the last single crochet; single crochet in the last single crochet, join with B in the top of beginning chain-3.

Round 16 With B, chain 1, single crochet in the same stitch, *double crochet in the next single crochet, single crochet in the next double crochet; repeat from * around, ending with double crochet in the last single crochet; join with A to first single crochet.

Round 17 With A, chain 1, single crochet in the same stitch, single crochet in each stitch around, join with B to first single crochet.

Round 18: *Child's Size Only* With B, chain 2, yarn over, insert the hook in the next stitch and pull up a loop, [yarn over, draw through 2 loops] twice (1 stitch decreased), work double crochet 2 together around— 6 stitches total.

Round 18: *Woman's Size Only* With B, chain 3, work double crochet 2 together around—7 stitches total.

Both Sizes Cut yarn leaving a long tail for sewing. With large-eyed, blunt needle thread tail and pull through remaining stitches. Pull tight to gather, fasten off securely. Weave in ends.

FLOWER

TOP

Round 1 With A, chain 3, join with a slip stitch to form a ring. Chain 5 (counts as 1 double crochet, chain 2), *double crochet in the ring, chain 2; repeat from * 3 times more, join to the 3rd chain of beginning chain-5—5 double crochet.

Round 2 Slip stitch in chain-2 space, (single crochet, 3 double crochet, single crochet) in same space, *(single crochet, 3 double crochet, single crochet) in each space around, *do not join*—5 petals.

BOTTOM

Round 1 With right side facing and working behind top petals, *chain 3, double crochet in the ring between the double crochet of top petals; repeat from * 5 times more, working last 2 double crochet between the same top petals. Join to the first chain of beginning chain-3, changing to B.

Round 2 Slip stitch in chain-3 space, (single crochet, 5 double crochet, single crochet) in the same space, *(single crochet, 5 double crochet, single crochet) in the next space; repeat from * around, join to the first single crochet and fasten off. With A, sew to band.

CENTER

Working with B on top, *insert hook in the center, catching a stitch; yarn over and draw up a loop, yarn over and draw up a long loop through the first loop; repeat from * twice more, leaving the long loops on the hook. Remove hook and fasten off.

7.
FELTED HATS

Everyone's felting! Felting tightens and shrinks knitted or crocheted fabric, making it firmer, stronger, and warmer. To make felt, you need wool or yarns with a high percentage of wool. Lion Brand Landscapes, which is used for I Felt Like It (page 86), has an acrylic core wrapped with wool. When it is washed, the wool felts around the acrylic, which gives the finished item an interesting texture and appearance. However, it does not felt exactly the same as 100% wool and may take longer to felt than pure wool.

When knitting or crocheting something you want to felt, you should use a larger needle or hook than you normally would for that yarn. Swatching is of the utmost importance. Make a large swatch (at least an 8" [20.5 cm] square) and felt it exactly as you plan to felt your finished project.

There are three factors necessary for successful felting: water, temperature change, and agitation. Felting can be done by hand, but it is much faster and easier to use a washing machine. Use a long wash setting with hot water and a cold rinse. Use your regular detergent and add several sturdy, washable items like jeans, clean canvas shoes, or tennis balls. Towels tend to embed lint into the felt so they should be avoided.

Regardless of the yarn you use, you may have to wash your project several times to felt it to your satisfaction. Felting is not an exact science and there are a number of variables that affect the rate of felting. The water temperature, whether you have hard or soft water, the detergent, and the amount of agitation will all make a difference. The size of your project will also play a role. Large pieces felt differently than small pieces. To felt additionally, dry by machine on the regular setting until almost dry.

After felting, remove your hat from the machine and place it over a round object to hold its shape while it dries. Some people are lucky enough to have a bowl or plastic container the size and shape of their head. If you do not, use a balloon.

Before felting.

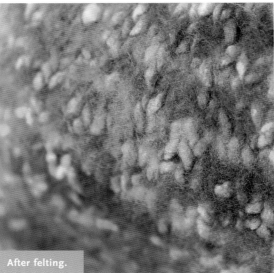

After felting.

I FELT LIKE IT

DESIGNED BY LINDA CYR

KNIT/INTERMEDIATE

Hats are great beginner felting projects because they knit up quick and can be shaped to fit a variety of head sizes—keep felting until it fits! This classic brimmed hat looks great on everyone.

SIZE (AFTER FELTING):
25" (63.5 cm) circumference x 6½" (16.5 cm) depth without brim; size is variable (see Finishing)

MATERIALS

LION BRAND LANDSCAPES
50% WOOL, 50% ACRYLIC
1¾ OZ (50 G) 55 YD (50 M) BALL

4 skeins #276 Summer Fields or color of your choice

• Size 10 (6 mm)—24" (61 cm) long circular needle *or size to obtain gauge*

• Size 10 (6 mm) double-pointed needles—set of four

• Stitch marker

• Large-eyed, blunt needle

GAUGE
11 stitches + 14 rows = 4" (10 cm) over stockinette stitch (knit every round) before felting.

Be sure to check your gauge.

NOTE
• Hat will shrink to finished measurements after felting.

HAT
With circular needle, cast on 106 stitches. Join work, being careful not to twist.

BRIM
Note The decrease round is worked in a constant spiral, instead of working separate rounds.
Decrease Round Working continuously, and ignoring the end of round, [knit 29, knit 2 together] 18 times—88 stitches total. Place marker to indicate end of round.

CROWN
Work even in reverse stockinette stitch (purl every round) for 6 rounds. Work even in stockinette stitch for 15 rounds.

CROWN SHAPING
Note Change to double-pointed needles when necessary.
Decrease Round 1 *Knit 6, knit 2 together; repeat from * around—77 stitches total.
Knit next round.
Decrease Round 2 *Knit 5, knit 2 together; repeat from * around—66 stitches total.
Knit next round.
Decrease Round 3 *Knit 4, knit 2 together; repeat from * around—55 stitches total.
Knit next round.
Decrease Round 4 *Knit 3, knit 2 together; repeat from * around—44 stitches total.
Knit next round.
Decrease Round 5 *Knit 2, knit 2 together; repeat from * around—33 stitches total.
Knit next round.
Decrease Round 6 *Knit 1, knit 2

together; repeat from * around—
22 stitches total.
Knit next round.
Decrease Round 7 [Knit 2 together]
11 times—11 stitches total.
Cut yarn leaving 10" (25.5 cm) tail.
Thread tail into large-eyed, blunt
needle, and pull through remaining
stitches. Pull to gather; then fasten
off securely.

FINISHING
FELTING
Machine wash hat, running
through two hot/cold cycles.
Machine-dry with dryer set on high.
Steam-block hat to desired size.

I FELT LIKE IT

CLARA BOW

DESIGNED BY LINDA CYR

CROCHET/INTERMEDIATE

Crocheters can felt too! Adorn this cloche with a chenille bow for old Hollywood glamour.

SIZE

23½" (60 cm) circumference x 7" (18 cm) depth without brim after felting; size is variable (see Finishing)

MATERIALS

 LION BRAND FISHERMEN'S WOOL
100% PURE VIRGIN WOOL
8 OZ (224 G) 465 YD (425 M) SKEIN

1 skein #098 Natural (MC)

 LION BRAND LION CHENILLE
100% ACRYLIC
3 OZ (85 G) 174 YD (157 M) BALL

1 ball #153 Black (CC) or color of your choice

- Size G-6 and I-9 (4 and 5.5 mm) crochet hooks *or size to obtain gauge*

- Small safety pin

- Black sewing thread and needle

- Straight pins

GAUGE

13 stitches = 4" (10 cm) over single crochet using MC and larger crochet hook, before felting.
Be sure to check your gauge.

NOTE

- Hat will shrink to finished measurements after felting.

HAT

Beginning at top of crown, with larger hook and MC, chain 2.
Round 1 Work 6 single crochet in the 2nd chain from the hook. You will be working in a spiral, marking the last stitch made with the safety pin to indicate the end of round.
Round 2 Work 2 single crochet in each stitch around—12 stitches total.
Round 3 *Single crochet in the next stitch, work 2 single crochet in the next stitch; repeat from * around—18 stitches total.

Round 4 *Single crochet in the next 2 stitches, work 2 single crochet in the next stitch; repeat from * around—24 stitches total.
Round 5 *Single crochet in the next 3 stitches, work 2 single crochet in the next stitch; repeat from * around—30 stitches total.
Round 6 *Single crochet in the next 4 stitches, work 2 single crochet in the next stitch; repeat from * around—36 stitches total.
Round 7 *Single crochet in the next 5 stitches, work 2 single crochet in the next stitch; repeat from * around—42 stitches total.
Round 8 *Single crochet in the next 6 stitches, work 2 single crochet in the next stitch; repeat from * around—48 stitches total.
Round 9 *Single crochet in the next 7 stitches, work 2 single crochet in the next stitch; repeat from * around—54 stitches total.

Round 10 *Single crochet in the next 8 stitches, work 2 single crochet in the next stitch; repeat from * around—60 stitches total.

Round 11 *Single crochet in the next 9 stitches, work 2 single crochet in the next stitch; repeat from * around—66 stitches total.

Round 12 *Single crochet in the next 10 stitches, work 2 single crochet in the next stitch; repeat from * around—72 stitches total.

Round 13 *Single crochet in the next 11 stitches, work 2 single crochet in the next stitch; repeat from * around—78 stitches total.

Rounds 14, 16, 18, 19 Single crochet in each stitch around.

Round 15 *Single crochet in the next 12 stitches, work 2 single crochet in the next stitch; repeat from * around—84 stitches total.

Round 17 *Single crochet in the next 13 stitches, work 2 single crochet in the next stitch; repeat from * around—90 stitches total.

Round 20 *Single crochet in the next 14 stitches, work 2 single crochet in the next stitch; repeat from * around—96 stitches total.

Rounds 21–23 Single crochet in each stitch around.

Round 24 *Single crochet in the next 15 stitches, work 2 single crochet in the next stitch; repeat from * around—102 stitches total.

Rounds 25–32 Single crochet in each stitch around.

Round 33 *Single crochet in the next 16 stitches, work 2 single crochet in the next stitch; repeat from * around—108 stitches total.

Rounds 34, 36, 38, 40 Single crochet in each stitch around.

Round 35 *Single crochet in the next 17 stitches, work 2 single crochet in the next stitch; repeat from * around—114 stitches total.

Round 37 *Single crochet in the next 18 stitches, work 2 single crochet in the next stitch; repeat from * around—120 stitches total.

Round 39 *Single crochet in the next 19 stitches, work 2 single crochet in the next stitch; repeat from * around—126 stitches total.

Round 41 *Single crochet in the next 20 stitches, work 2 single crochet in the next stitch; repeat from * around—132 stitches total.

Round 42 Slip stitch in each stitch around. Fasten off.

FINISHING

FELTING

Machine-wash hat, running through two hot/cold cycles. Machine-dry with dryer set on high. Block hat to desired size.

HATBAND

With smaller hook and CC, chain 11.

Row 1 Single crochet in the 2nd chain from the hook and in each chain across—10 stitches total. Chain 1, turn.

Row 2 Single crochet in each stitch across. Chain 1, turn.

Repeat Row 2 for pattern stitch and work even until piece measures 36" (91 cm) long. Fasten off. Weave in ends.

Using sewing needle and thread, sew ends of hatband together. Pin hatband around hat. Form bow by tacking excess hatband material in place. Tie a strand of CC tightly around the center of the bow to shape. Tack hatband to hat along the top edge only.

8.

GREAT PATTERNS

Put your stitching skills to use by making these fashionable hats. The patterns in this chapter may involve a few new maneuvers for some, but rest assured you'll be pleased with the results. From bobbles and pom-poms to cables and earflaps—we've got you covered. Rebel Rebel (page 94) and Urban Trekker (opposite) are so stylish they may be your inspiration to learn cabling if you don't know how. Those who yearn for extra ear coverage during winter months should whip up a Swiss Miss (page 96) or a Paul Bunyan (page 99). The Long and Short of It (page 102) and Carrie's Cap (page 105) are both crocheter's delights. With so many choices, it'll be difficult to choose just one to start.

URBAN TREKKER

DESIGNED BY VLADIMIR TERIOKHIN

KNIT/INTERMEDIATE

Start at the top and knit down to make this topper just the right size. The smooth wool-blend yarn showcases allover cables to perfection.

SIZE

S/M (M/L)

18" (20") / 45.5 (51) cm circumference x 9" (10") / 23 (25.5) cm depth without earflaps

MATERIALS

LION BRAND KOOL WOOL
50% MERINO WOOL, 50% ACRYLIC
1³/₄ OZ (50 G) 60 YD (54 M) BALL

3 balls #113 Tomato or color of your choice

- For size S/M, size 10 (6 mm) knitting needles *or size to obtain gauge*

- For size M/L, size 10.5 (6.5 mm) knitting needles *or size to obtain gauge*

- For size S/M, size 10 (6 mm) double-pointed needles—set of four

- For size M/L, size 10.5 (6.5 mm) double-pointed needles—set of four

- Cable needle

- Stitch holder

- Stitch marker

- Large-eyed, blunt needle

- Pieces of cardboard 2¹/₂" (6.5 cm) and 3" (7.5 cm) wide

GAUGE

20 stitches + 22 rounds = 4" (10 cm) over Cable Pattern using size 10 (6 mm) needles
18 stitches +20 rounds = 4" (10 cm) over Cable Pattern using size 10.5 (6.5 mm) needles
Be sure to check your gauge.

STITCH EXPLANATIONS

4-stitch Right Cross Slip 2 stitches to cable needle and hold in back, knit 2, knit 2 from the cable needle.

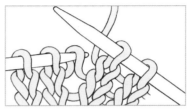

1. Insert tip of left needle under the strand between the two needles.

2. To make one as if to knit, knit into the back of the stitch.

3. To make one as if to purl, purl into the back of the stitch.

6-stitch Right Cross Slip 3 stitches to cable needle and hold in back, knit 3, knit 3 from cable needle.

Make 1 (make 1 stitch as if to knit) An increase worked by moving the left needle from front to back to pick up the horizontal thread lying between the needles and placing it onto the left needle (illustration 1). Work this new stitch by knitting through the back loop (illustration 2).

Make 1 Purl (make 1 stitch as if to purl) An increase worked by lifting the horizontal thread lying between the needles and placing it onto the left needle. Purl this new stitch through the back loop (illustration 3).

HAT

Beginning at the top of the crown, cast on 10 stitches. Divide stitches between 3 double-pointed needles. Join and place marker to mark the beginning of the round.

Round 1 Knit.

Round 2 *Knit 1, make 1; repeat from * around—20 stitches total.

Round 3 *Purl 1, knit 1; repeat from * around.

Round 4 *Purl 1, knit 1, make 1; repeat from * around—30 stitches total.

Rounds 5–8 *Purl 1, knit 2; repeat from * around.

Round 9 *Purl 1, [knit 1, make 1] twice; repeat from * around—50 stitches total.

Round 10 *Purl 1, 4-stitch Right Cross; repeat from * around.

Round 11 *Purl 1, knit 1, make 1, knit 2, make 1, knit 1; repeat from * around—70 stitches total.

Rounds 12–17 *Purl 1, knit 6; repeat from * around.

Round 18 *Purl 1, 6-stitch Right Cross; repeat from * around.

Round 19 *Purl 1, make 1 Purl, knit 6; repeat from * around—80 stitches total.

Rounds 20–25 *Purl 2, knit 6; repeat from * around.

Round 26 *Purl 2, 6-stitch Right Cross; repeat from * around.

Round 27 *Purl 2, make 1 Purl, knit 6; repeat from * around—90 stitches total.

Rounds 28–33 *Purl 3, knit 6; repeat from * around.

Round 34 *Purl 3, 6-stitch Right Cross; repeat from * around.

Rounds 35–41 Repeat Round 28.

Round 42 Repeat Round 34.

Rounds 43–45 Repeat Round 28.

Rounds 46–49 [Knit 1, purl 1] 15 times, [knit 6, purl 3] 6 times, knit 6.

Round 50 Bind off first 30 stitches as if to purl (the front of hat), [6-stitch Right Cross, purl 3] 6 times, 6-stitch Right Cross—60 stitches. Change to straight needles and work back and forth.

Rows 51, 53 and 55 (Wrong Side) [Purl 6, knit 3] 6 times, purl 6.

Rows 52 and 54 [Knit 6, purl 3] 6 times, knit 6.

Row 56 (Right Side) [Knit 6, purl 3] twice, knit 4, slip these stitches onto holder for left earflap, bind off next 16 stitches as if to purl (the

back of hat), knit 4, [purl 3, knit 6] twice—22 stitches total.

RIGHT EARFLAP

Row 57 (Wrong Side) [Purl 6, knit 3] twice, purl 4.

Row 58 Knit 2 together, knit 2, purl 3, 6-stitch Right Cross, purl 3, knit 4, knit 2 together—20 stitches total.

Row 59 Purl 5, knit 3, purl 6, knit 3, purl 3. Continue to work 6-stitch Right Cross every 8th row once more. AT THE SAME TIME, decrease 1 stitch each side on the next row, then every other row 8 times more, ending with a wrong side row—2 stitches.

Last Row (Right Side) Knit 2 together. Fasten off last stitch.

LEFT EARFLAP

Slip 22 stitches from the holder onto the needle ready for a wrong side row.

Row 57 (Wrong Side) Purl 4, [knit 3, purl 6] twice.

Row 58 Knit 2 together, knit 4, purl 3, 6-stitch Right Cross, purl 3, knit 2, knit 2 together—20 stitches total.

Row 59 Purl 3, knit 3, purl 6, knit 3, purl 5. Continue to work same as for right earflap.

FINISHING

Cut a strand of yarn about 10" (25.5 cm) in length. Thread into large-eyed, blunt needle, and weave through remaining stitches at the top of the crown. Pull tight to gather stitches to close the top of the hat, fasten off securely.

TIES

For each tie, cut 3 lengths of yarn, 15" (38 cm) each. Thread strands through the bottom point of the earflap. Working strands in pairs, braid tightly for 9" (23 cm). Knot ends close to braid. Do not cut excess yarn.

POM-POMS—MAKE 2 OF 2¹/₂" (6.5 CM) DIAMETER, 1 OF 3" (7.5 CM)

Follow directions for pom-pom on page 14.

Using 2 strands of excess yarn from tie, sew the smaller pom-pom to the end of one tie. Thread remaining ends into large-eyed, blunt needle and draw through center of pom-pom to incorporate them. Trim ends even with pom-pom. Repeat for other tie. Sew larger pom-pom to top of hat.

REBEL REBEL

DESIGNED BY LIDIA KARABINECH

KNIT/INTERMEDIATE

The cables continue right off this easy-to-knit, fun-to-wear topper. Perfect guy or gal garb!

SIZE
S/M (M/L)
20½" (21½") / 52 (54.5) cm circumference x 7" (8") / 18 (20.5) cm depth

MATERIALS

LION BRAND WOOL-EASE CHUNKY
80% ACRYLIC, 20% WOOL
5 OZ (140 G) 153 YD (140 M) BALL

1 ball #152 Charcoal or color of your choice

- Size 10.5 (6.5 mm) 16" (40.5 cm) long circular needle *or size to obtain gauge*

- Cable needle

- Stitch holders

- Stitch markers

- Large-eyed, blunt needle

- 3½" x 3½" (9 x 9 cm) piece of cardboard

GAUGE
14 stitches = 4" (10 cm) over stockinette stitch (knit every round).
Be sure to check your gauge.

STITCH EXPLANATIONS
Make 1 An increase worked by moving the left needle from front to back to pick up the horizontal thread lying between needles. Work this new stitch by knitting through the back loop (see page 91).

PATTERN STITCHES
CABLE PATTERN IN THE ROUND (WORKED OVER 8 STITCHES)
Rounds 1 and 2 Knit 8.
Round 3 Slip 4 stitches to cable needle and hold in front, knit 4, knit 4 from cable needle.
Rounds 4–6 Knit 8.
Repeat Rounds 1–6 for Cable Pattern in the round.

CABLE PATTERN IN ROWS (WORKED OVER 8 STITCHES)
Rows 1 and 5 (Right Side) Knit 8.
Row 3 Slip 4 stitches to cable needle and hold in front, knit 4, knit 4 from the cable needle.
Rows 2, 4, and 6 Purl 8.
Repeat Rows 1–6 for cable pattern in rows.

HAT
Cast on 72 (76) stitches. Join work and place marker to mark beginning of round.
Work in knit 1, purl 1 rib for 4 rounds.
Next (Increase) Round Knit 15 (16), place marker for cable, knit 1, make 1, knit 2, make 1, knit 2, make 1, place marker, knit 31 (33), place marker for cable, knit 1, make 1, knit 2, make 1, knit 2, make 1, place marker, knit 16 (17)—78 (86) stitches total.

Begin Cable Pattern

Round 1 Knit 15 (16), slip marker, knit 8, slip marker, knit 31 (33), slip marker, knit 8, slip marker, knit 16 (17). Keeping the stitches between the cables in stockinette stitch, work cable pattern in the round as established until piece measures 7" (8") / 18 (20 cm) from beginning.

CABLE BRAIDS

Next Round Bind off 15 (16) stitches, knit 8 then place stitches on holder, bind off next 31 (33) stitches, knit 8 then place stitches on holder, bind off last 16 (17) stitches. Slip 8 stitches from holder to needle ready for a wrong side row. Work in cable pattern in rows as established for 3" (7.5 cm). Cut yarn leaving a long tail for sewing. Thread tail into large-eyed, blunt needle, and pull through remaining stitches. Pull tight to gather, fasten off securely, then sew edges together. Slip 8 stitches from the remaining holder to needle ready for a wrong side row. Work same as for the first braid.

FINISHING

Sew top seam. Make two tassels following directions on page 14. Sew tassels to ends.

REBEL REBEL

SWISS MISS HAT

DESIGNED BY VLADIMIR TERIOKHAN

CROCHET/EASY

Oversized pom-poms make fun, unique earflaps on this comfortable crocheted hat.

SIZE

17½" (44.5 cm) circumference x 7½" (19 cm) depth without earflaps

MATERIALS

LION BRAND KOOL WOOL
50% MERINO WOOL, 50% ACRYLIC
1¾ OZ (50 G) 60 YD (54 M) BALL

3 balls #098 Ivory or color of your choice

- Size K-10.5 (6.5 mm) crochet hook *or size to obtain gauge*

- Large-eyed, blunt needle

- 3½" x 3½" (9 cm x 9 cm) Cardboard for pom-poms

GAUGE

11 double crochet + 6 rows = 4" (10 cm).
Be sure to check your gauge.

NOTES

- Hat is started at the crown and worked down.

- Earflaps are worked separately, then sewn on.

- Join every round of hat with a slip stitch in the first single crochet or top of beginning chain-3.

- Beginning chain-1 for single crochet rows does not count as a single crochet.

STITCH EXPLANATION

Bobble Work all in same stitch: [Yarn over, insert hook in stitch and draw up a loop, yarn over and draw through 2 loops] 4 times, yarn over, draw through all loops on hook—1 bobble made.

HAT

Chain 3, join with a slip stitch in the first chain to form a ring.
Round 1 Chain 1, work 9 single crochet in the ring; join—9 single crochet.
Round 2 Chain 3 (counts as 1 double crochet), double crochet in same stitch, work 2 double crochet in each single crochet around; join—18 double crochet.
Round 3 Chain 3, *2 double crochet in the next double crochet, 1 double crochet in the next double crochet; repeat from * around, working the last double crochet in the same stitch as the beginning chain-3; join—28 double crochet.
Round 4 Chain 3, *1 double crochet in the next double crochet, 2 double crochet in the next double crochet; repeat from * around to last stitch, 1 double crochet in the last stitch, 1 double crochet in the same stitch as the beginning chain-3; join—42 double crochet.
Round 5 Chain 3, 1 double crochet in each of the next 2 double crochet; *2 double crochet in the next double crochet, 1 double crochet in each of the next 6 double crochet; repeat from * around, to last 4 stitches, 1 double crochet in each

of the next 4 double crochet, 1 double crochet in the same stitch as the beginning chain-3; join—48 double crochet.

Round 6 Chain 3, double crochet in each double crochet around; join.

Round 7 Chain 1, single crochet in the same stitch and in each double crochet around; join—48 single crochet.

Round 8 Chain 3, double crochet in each of the next 4 single crochet, *chain 1, skip the next single crochet, bobble in the next single crochet, chain 1, skip 1 single crochet, double crochet in each of the next 5 single crochet; repeat from * around to last 3 stitches, chain 1, skip 1 single crochet, bobble in the next single crochet, chain 1; skip last single crochet, join—6 bobbles.

Round 9 Chain 1, single crochet in the same stitch, single crochet in each stitch and chain-1 space around; join.

Round 10 Chain 3, double crochet in the next single crochet, *chain 1, skip 1 single crochet, bobble in the next single crochet, chain 1, skip 1 single crochet, double crochet in each of the next 5 single crochet; repeat from * around to the last 6 stitches; chain 1, skip 1 single crochet, bobble in the next single crochet, chain 1, skip 1 single crochet, double crochet in each of the next 3 single crochet; join.

Round 11 Repeat Round 9.

Round 12 Repeat Round 8.

Round 13 Repeat Round 9.

Round 14 Chain 3, double crochet in each stitch around; join—48 double crochet.

Round 15 Repeat Round 9. Fasten off.

EARFLAPS—MAKE 2

Row 1 (Right Side) Chain 4, 6 double crochet in the first chain. Turn.

Row 2 Chain 3, 2 double crochet in each of the next 5 double crochet, double crochet in the next double crochet—12 double crochet. Turn.

Row 3 Chain 1, single crochet in the first stitch, [2 single crochet in the next double crochet, single crochet in each of the next 3 double crochet] twice, single crochet in next double crochet, 2 single crochet in the next double crochet, single crochet in the top of the turning chain. Fasten off. Weave in ends.

FINISHING

Sew earflaps to the bottom edge of hat, spaced 4" (10 cm) apart at the back of the hat and 7" (18 cm) apart at the front of the hat.

SMALL TASSELS—MAKE 2

Following directions on page 14, make two tassels 6" (15 cm) long using seven strands of yarn each.

LARGE TASSELS—MAKE 2

Make same as for the small tassels, but using 11 strands of yarn each.

TIES

Join to earflap with slip stitch between the 2 center double crochet, leaving approximately 18" (46 cm) tail. Chain 64, fasten off. Sew tie to the top of the small tassel. Sew 18" (46 cm) tail to top of the large tassel. Repeat on other earflap.

POM-POMS—MAKE 3

Following directions of page 14, make 3 pom-poms 3½" (9 cm) in diameter. Sew to crown of hat and at the center of each earflap. Do not cut tails. For each tail, thread onto large-eyed, blunt needle, then insert through the center of the pom-pom to incorporate it into pom-pom. Trim tails even with pom-poms.

PAUL BUNYAN

DESIGNED BY DORIS CHAN

CROCHET/INTERMEDIATE

This is a luxurious take on the traditional lumberjack hat made in a bulky wool-blend yarn and trimmed with chenille. The flaps flip down for extra warmth.

SIZE
S/M (M/L)
21–22" (22–23") [53.5–56 (56–58.5) cm] circumference x 7" (18 cm) depth

MATERIALS

LION BRAND WOOL-EASE THICK & QUICK
80% ACRYLIC, 20% WOOL
6 OZ (170 G) 108 YD (98 M) BALL

1 ball #413 Lumberjack Red (MC) or color of your choice

LION BRAND CHENILLE THICK & QUICK
91% ACRYLIC, 9% RAYON
5.6 OZ (158 G) 100 YD (91.5 M) SKEINS

1 skein #153 Black (CC) or color of your choice

• Size P-15 (10 mm) crochet hook
  or size to obtain gauge

• Scrap of contrasting yarn for marker

GAUGE
7 stitches = 4" (10 cm) over single crochet using MC.
Be sure to check your gauge.

NOTES
• The hat is crocheted from the top down, the visor and earflaps are added later.

• Single crochet in the round, right side always facing.

• Earflaps may be worn down and tied under the chin or flipped up and tied above hat. The visor also can be worn up or down.

STITCH EXPLANATIONS
Front post single crochet: Working from front to back to front, insert the hook around the post of the stitch of the row below, yarn over and draw up a loop, yarn over and draw through 2 loops on the hook.

Single crochet 2 together (single crochet decrease): Insert the hook into a stitch and draw up a loop. Insert the hook into the next stitch and draw up a loop. Yarn over, draw through all 3 loops on hook (see page 11).

Single crochet 3 together: Insert the hook into a stitch and draw up a loop. (Insert hook into the next stitch and draw up a loop) twice. Yarn over, draw through all 4 loops on hook.

HAT
CROWN
Round 1 With MC, chain 2, work 6 single crochet in the 2nd chain from the hook. Join, placing marker. Continue working in the round.

Round 2 Work 2 single crochet in each stitch—12 stitches total.

Round 3 *Single crochet in the next

stitch, work 2 single crochet in the next stitch; repeat from * around—18 stitches total.

Round 4 *Single crochet in the next 2 stitches, work 2 single crochet in the next stitch; repeat from * around—24 stitches total.

Round 5 *Single crochet in the next 3 stitches, work 2 single crochet in the next stitch; repeat from * around—30 stitches total.

Round 6 *Single crochet in the next 4 stitches, work 2 single crochet in the next stitch; repeat from * around—36 stitches total.

For size Medium/Large only

Round 7 [Single crochet in the next 11 stitches, work 2 single crochet in the next stitch] 3 times—39 stitches total.

BODY

Work even on 36 (39) stitches for 8 more rounds, or until hat measures 7" (7½") [18 (19) cm] long. (**Note** Visor and earflaps are worked back and forth on part of the body stitches. First make a turning row of single crochet around the front post.)

Turning Row

Next Row (Right Side) With MC, front post single crochet in the next 28 (30) stitches. Turn.

LEFT EARFLAP

Row 1 (Wrong Side) Chain 1, working through back loops only, single crochet in the first 6 (7) stitches. Turn.

Row 2 Chain 1, single crochet in each stitch. Turn.

Rows 3–5 Repeat Row 2.

Row 6 Chain 1, single crochet 2 together, single crochet in the next 2 (3) stitches, single crochet 2 together—4 (5) stitches total. Turn.

Rows 7–8 Repeat Row 2.

Row 9 Chain 1, single crochet 2 together, single crochet in the next 0 (1) stitch, single crochet 2 together—2 (3) stitches total. Turn.

For size Medium/Large only

Row 10 Repeat Row 2.

For all sizes

Last Row Chain 1, single crochet 2 together (single crochet 3 together)—1 stitch. Fasten off.

VISOR

On the wrong side of the turning row, skip the next stitch from the left earflap, then join MC with a slip stitch in the back loop of the next stitch.

Row 1 Chain 1, working through back loops only, single crochet in the same stitch as joining, single

crochet in the next 4 stitches, work 2 single crochet in the next stitch, single crochet in the next 2 stitches, work 2 single crochet in the next stitch, single crochet in the next 5 stitches—16 stitches total. Turn.

Row 2 Chain 1, single crochet 2 together over the first 2 stitches, single crochet in the next 12 stitches, single crochet 2 together over the last 2 stitches—14 stitches total. Turn.

Row 3 Chain 1, single crochet 2 together over the first 2 stitches, single crochet in the next 3 stitches, work 2 single crochet in the next stitch, single crochet in the next 2 stitches, work 2 single crochet in the next stitch, single crochet in the next 3 stitches, single crochet 2 together over the last 2 stitches—14 stitches total. Turn.

Row 4 Chain 1, single crochet 2 together over the first 2 stitches, single crochet in the next 10 stitches, single crochet 2 together over the last 2 stitches—12 stitches total. Turn.

Row 5 Chain 1, single crochet 2 together over the first 2 stitches, single crochet in the next 2 stitches, work 2 single crochet in the next stitch, single crochet in the next 2 stitches, work 2 single crochet in the next stitch, single crochet in the next 2 stitches, single crochet 2 together over the last 2 stitches—12 stitches total. Turn. **Row 6** Chain 1, single crochet 2 together over the first 2 stitches, single crochet in the next 8 stitches, single crochet 2 together over the last 2 stitches—10 single crochet total. Fasten off.

RIGHT EARFLAP
On the wrong side of the turning row, skip the next stitch from visor, then join MC with a slip stitch in the back loop of the next stitch. Work same as for left earflap.

LININGS
Visor and earflaps are lined on the inside (toward your face). Using CC, work same as left earflap, visor, and right earflap, working the first row of each piece through the front loop of the turning row.

FINISHING
Weave in ends.

JOINING
This last round joins the pieces to their linings, makes the ties at the tip of each earflap and adjusts the back of hat for fit. When joining pieces, hold with wrong sides together, matching rows, single crochet through both thicknesses, working under one strand of earflap or visor and one strand of lining, except as noted. **Note** If you find it difficult to insert the hook into the edges of the pieces, try a smaller hook for the joining and work loosely, but use the P-15 (10 mm) hook to make the ties.
With right side facing and CC, start at the right earflap. Join CC with a slip stitch through both loops of single crochet of turning row at the beginning of the earflap. Single crochet together the edge of the right earflap with lining, working one single crochet in each row—9 (10) stitches total. Rotate, then single crochet together the single crochet at the tip through both loops of each piece. Make the first tie as follows: chain 25, slip stitch in 2nd chain from hook, slip stitch in each chain, slip stitch down through the top of the single crochet at the base of the chain. Rotate, then single crochet together down the earflap—9 (10) stitches total. Slip stitch in both loops of the turning row at the end of the earflap, slip stitch in both loops of skipped single crochet of the turning row, slip stitch in both loops of the turning row at the beginning of the visor. Single crochet together visor and lining, working one single crochet in each row—6 stitches total. Rotate, then single crochet together at the front through both loops of each piece—10 stitches total. Rotate, single crochet together down the visor—6 stitches total. Slip stitch in both loops of the turning row, slip stitch in both loops in skipped single crochet of the turning row, slip stitch in both loops of the turning row at the beginning of the left earflap. Single crochet together and make the second tie same as the right earflap. Slip stitch in both loops of the turning row at the end of the left earflap, slip stitch in each 8 (9) stitches to beginning of round. Fasten off. **Note** Circumference of hat will "give" after some wear. Work the last 8 (9) slip stitches loosely if the fit is acceptable. Work the slip stitches firmly to make the hat a bit tighter if necessary.

THE LONG AND SHORT OF IT

DESIGNED BY LINDA CYR

CROCHET/INTERMEDIATE

The elongated brim of this ultra-fashionable hat can be worn long and loose or wrapped around your neck like a scarf.

SIZE

21" (53.5 cm) circumference x 7½" (19 cm) depth without earflaps

MATERIALS

 LION BRAND HOMESPUN 98% ACRYLIC, 2% POLYESTER 6 OZ (170 G) 185 YD (167 M) SKEIN

1 skein each #367 Covered Bridge Red (A), #371 Boston Rose (B), #370 Coral Gables (C), #372 Sunshine State (D), or colors of your choice

- Size I-9 (5.5 mm) crochet hook *or size to obtain gauge*

- Safety pin

GAUGE

14 stitches + 14 rounds = 4" (10 cm) over single crochet.
Be sure to check your gauge.

HAT

Beginning at the top of the crown, with A, chain 2.

Round 1 Work 6 single crochet in the 2nd chain from the hook. You will be working in a spiral, marking the last stitch made with the safety pin to indicate the end of the round.

Round 2 Work 2 single crochet in each stitch around—12 stitches total.

Round 3 *Single crochet in the next stitch, work 2 single crochet in the next stitch; repeat from * around—18 stitches total.

Round 4 *Single crochet in the next 2 stitches, work 2 single crochet in the next stitch; repeat from * around—24 stitches total.

Round 5 *Single crochet in the next 3 stitches, work 2 single crochet in the next stitch; repeat from * around—30 stitches total.

Round 6 *Single crochet in the next 4 stitches, work 2 single crochet in the next stitch; repeat from * around—36 stitches total.

Round 7 *Single crochet in the next 5 stitches, work 2 single crochet in the next stitch; repeat from * around—42 stitches total.

Round 8 Repeat Round 7—49 stitches total.

Round 9 *Single crochet in the next 6 stitches, work 2 single crochet in the next stitch; repeat from * around—56 stitches total.

Round 10 Single crochet in each stitch around.

Round 11 *Single crochet in the next 7 stitches, work 2 single crochet in the next stitch; repeat from * around—63 stitches total.

Round 12 *Single crochet in the next 8 stitches, work 2 single crochet in the next stitch; repeat from * around—70 stitches total.

Round 13 Single crochet in each stitch around.

Round 14 *Single crochet in the next 13 stitches, work 2 single crochet in the next stitch; repeat from * around—75 stitches total.

Rounds 15 and 16 Single crochet in each stitch around.

Round 17 *Single crochet in the next 14 stitches, work 2 single crochet in the next stitch; repeat from * around—80 stitches total.

Round 18 Slip stitch in each stitch around. Fasten off.

BRIM

With B, chain 263.

Row 1 Single crochet in the 2nd chain from the hook and in the next 103 chain, *[work 2 single crochet in the next chain, single crochet in the next 4 chain] 3 times, work 2 single crochet in the next chain**, single crochet in the next 22 chain; repeat from * to ** once more, end single crochet in last 104 chain—270 stitches total. Chain 1, turn.

Row 2 Single crochet in each stitch across. Join C, chain 1, turn.

Row 3 Single crochet in the first 106 stitches, *[work 2 single crochet in the next stitch, single crochet in the next 4 stitches] 3 times, work 2 single crochet in the next stitch**, single crochet in the next 26 stitches; repeat from * to ** once more, end single crochet in last 106 stitches—278 stitches total. Chain 1, turn.

Row 4 Single crochet in each stitch across. Join D, chain 1, turn.

Row 5 Single crochet in the first 108 stitches, *[work 2 single crochet in the next stitch, single crochet in the next 4 stitches] 3 times, work 2 single crochet in the next stitch**, single crochet in the next 30 stitches; repeat from * to ** once more, end single crochet in the last 108 stitches—286 stitches total. Chain 1, turn.

Row 6 Single crochet in each stitch across. Join A, chain 1, turn.

Row 7 Single crochet in the first 110 stitches, *[work 2 single crochet in the next stitch, single crochet in the next 4 stitches] 3 times, work 2 single crochet in the next stitch**, single crochet in the next 34 stitches; repeat from * to **, end single crochet in the last 110 stitches—294 stitches total.

Row 8 Single crochet in each stitch across. Do not chain, turn.

Row 9 Slip stitch in each stitch across. Fasten off.

FINISHING

Position the curved section of the brim over the front of the hat so both curved edges line up; brim tails will form earflaps. Carefully tack brim in place.

BRAID

Cut 2 strands, each 24" (61 cm) long, of B, C and D. Draw the strands through the top of the hat, so they are doubled. Group the colors together, then braid for 5" (12.5 cm). Tie ends with an overhand knot close to braid. Trim ends.

CARRIE'S CAP

DESIGNED BY VLADIMIR TERIOKHAN

CROCHET/INTERMEDIATE

You'll be tickled pink crocheting (and wearing) this take on a modern cult classic.

SIZE

21" (53.5 cm) circumference x 7½" (19 cm) depth

MATERIALS

5 BULKY LION BRAND JIFFY
100% ACRYLIC
3 OZ (85 G) 135 YD (123 M) BALL

2 balls #146 Fuchsia or color of your choice

- Size K-10.5 (6.5 mm) crochet hook *or size to obtain gauge*

- Large-eyed, blunt needle

GAUGE

First 3 rounds = 3.75" (9.5 cm) in diameter.
Be sure to check your gauge.

STITCH EXPLANATIONS

Cluster [Yarn over, insert hook in space/ring, yarn over, bring up a loop] 3 times—*7 loops on hook;* yarn over, draw through all loops on hook.

Double Cluster [Cluster, chain 1, cluster] in same space.

Single crochet 2 together through back loop (single crochet decrease) Insert the hook into the back loop of a stitch and draw up a loop. Insert the hook into the back loop of the next stitch and draw up a loop. Yarn over, draw through all 3 loops on hook (see page 11).

CAP

Chain 4, join with slip stitch to form a ring.

Round 1 (Cluster, chain 1) 8 times into the ring. Join round with a slip stitch in the top of the first cluster.

Round 2 Slip stitch in the first chain-space. (double cluster, chain 1) in each chain-space around— 8 double clusters. Join with slip stitch in top of first cluster.

Round 3 Slip stitch in first chain-space. (Double cluster in the chain-space at the center of double cluster, single crochet through the back loop in the top of the next cluster, 2 single crochet in the next chain) 8 times—8 double clusters, 3 single crochet in each section. Join with slip stitch in the top of the first cluster.

Round 4 (Increase Round) Slip stitch in the first chain-space. (Double cluster in chain-space at the center of the double cluster, single crochet through the back loop in the top of the next cluster, single crochet through the back loop in each single crochet to the next double cluster) 8 times—8 double clusters, 4 single crochet in each section. Join with slip stitch in the top of the first cluster.

Rounds 5–10 Repeat Round 4 for 6 times—8 double clusters, 10 single crochet in each section.

Rounds 11–12 Slip stitch in the first chain-space, (double cluster in the chain-space at the center of the double cluster, single crochet through the back loop in each single crochet to the next double cluster) 8 times. Join with slip stitch in the top of the first cluster.

Round 13 Slip stitch in the first chain-space. *Double cluster in the chain-space at the center of the double cluster, (single crochet 2 together through the back loop, single crochet through back loop in the next 2 single crochet) twice, single crochet 2 together through the back loop; repeat from * 7 times more—8 double clusters, 7 single crochet in each section.

Round 14 Single crochet through the back loop around, working single crochet 2 together through the back loop over each double cluster—56 single crochet, 8 single crochet decreases.

Rounds 15–19 Single crochet through both loops around.

Join round with slip stitch to the first single crochet of the round. Fasten off.

BRIM

Chain 9.

Round 1 Single crochet in the 2nd chain from the hook and in the next 6 chain, 3 single crochet in the last chain. Rotate to work across the bottom of the foundation chain. Single crochet in the the next chain, 2 single crochet in the last chain—18 single crochet total.

Round 2 (Single crochet in each of the next 8 single crochet, 3 single crochet in the next single crochet) twice—22 single crochet total.

Round 3 Single crochet in each of the next 9 single crochet, 3 single crochet in the next single crochet; single crochet in each of the next 10 single crochet, 3 single crochet in the next single crochet, single crochet in the next single crochet—26 single crochet total.

Round 4 Single crochet in each of the next 10 single crochet, 3 single crochet in the next single crochet; single crochet in each of the next 12 single crochet, 3 single crochet in the next single crochet, single crochet in the next 2 single crochet—30 single crochet total.

Round 5 Single crochet in each of the next 11 single crochet, 3 single crochet in the next single crochet; single crochet in each of the next 14 single crochet, 3 single crochet in the next single crochet, single crochet in the next 3 single crochet—34 single crochet total.

Round 6 Single crochet in each of the next 12 single crochet, 3 single crochet in the next single crochet; single crochet in each of the next 16 single crochet, 3 single crochet in the next single crochet, single crochet in each of the the next 4 single crochet—38 single crochets total.

Round 7 Single crochet in each of the next 13 single crochet, 3 single crochet in the the next single crochet; single crochet in each of next 18 single crochet, 3 single crochet in the next single crochet, single crochet in each of the next 5 single crochet—42 single crochet total. Join with slip stitch to the first single crochet. Fasten off. Weave in ends.

FINISHING

Flatten brim so the increases are at the side edges. Center brim across 2 sections of the cap, with one double cluster at each edge and one at the center. Sew brim firmly to Round 14 of cap.

GLOSSARY

BACK POST DOUBLE CROCHET (BPDC): Yarn over, insert hook from back to front then to back, going around the double crochet post, draw up a loop (yarn over and draw through 2 loops on hook) twice. Skip stitch in front of the BPDC.

CC: Contrast color in a two-color scarf.

CHAIN: In crocheting, this is a loop made simply by drawing the yarn through an existing stitch or loop. It also refers to a series of loops; "chain 3" means to make three chain stitches in a row.

CN: Cable needle.

DOUBLE CROCHET (DC): This is a basic crochet stitch that is taller than a half double and shorter than a triple crochet stitch.

FRONT POST DOUBLE CROCHET (FPDC): Yarn over, insert hook from front to back then to front, going around the double crochet post, draw up a loop, (yarn over and draw through 2 loops on hook) twice. Skip stitch behind the FPDC.

GARTER STITCH: Knit every row.

GAUGE: Sometimes called tension, gauge is the number of stitches and rows measured over a number of inches (or centimeters).

GRAFTING: A technique for joining two rows of "live" stitches without a seam. To graft, hold the two needles with the live stitches on them parallel with wrong sides of fabric together. Thread a blunt tapestry needle with one of the yarn ends and work as follows: Insert tapestry needle as if to purl into the first stitch on the front piece. Insert needle as if to knit into the first stitch on the back piece. Then follow steps 1–4 as outlined below. (1) Insert needle as if to knit through the first stitch on front knitting needle and let the stitch drop from the needle. (2) Insert tapestry needle into 2nd stitch on the front needle as if to purl and pull the yarn through, leaving stitch on the knitting needle. (3) Insert tapestry needle into the first stitch on the back needle as if to purl and let it drop from the knitting needle, then (4) insert tapestry needle as if to knit through 2nd stitch on back needle and pull the yarn through, leaving the stitch on the knitting needle. Repeat 1–4 until all stitches are gone. When finished, adjust the tension as necessary. Weave in ends.

HALF DOUBLE CROCHET: A crochet stitch that is taller than a single crochet and shorter than double crochet.

KNIT 2 TOGETHER (K2TOG): A decrease made by inserting the needle into the first two stitches on the left needle, wrapping the yarn around as you normally would, and then pulling the yarn through both stitches. See illustrations on page 76.

LEFT-SLANTED DECREASE: See knit 2 together.

MAKE 1: An increase worked by lifting the horizontal thread lying between the needles and placing it on the left needle. Work this new stitch through the back loop.

MC: Main color in a two-color scarf.

RIGHT-SLANTED DECREASE: See slip, slip, knit.

SINGLE CROCHET (SC): A basic crochet stitch that is taller than a slip stitch and shorter than a half double crochet.

SLIDE: Push stitches back to opposite end of needle and, keeping the same side of the fabric facing, work the next row.

SLIP, SLIP, KNIT (SSK): Slip next two stitches as if to knit, one at a time, to the right needle; insert left needle into the fronts of these two stitches and knit them together. See illustrations on page 76.

S2KP2: Slip 2 sts as if to knit, knit 1, pass 2 slipped stitches over.

STOCKINETTE STITCH: Knit one row, purl one row.

TRIPLE (TREBLE) CROCHET: This is the tallest of all the basic crochet stitches.

TURN: Turn needle around and, with opposite side of fabric facing, work the next row.

WHIPSTITCH: A decorative seaming technique. Using either matching or contrasting yarn, bring needle through the fabric of one piece to be joined from wrong side to right side. Insert needle back through the fabric of the other piece and pull yarn carefully, avoiding pulling stitches too tightly. Repeat to end of fabric.

YARN OVER (YO): An increase created by wrapping the yarn counterclockwise around the right-hand needle and knitting the next stitch.

BABKA HAT, PAGE 39

BASIC CROCHET HAT WITH
DOUBLE CROCHET RIB, PAGE 29

BASIC CROCHET HAT WITH
TOP KNOT, PAGE 28

BASIC CROCHET HAT WITH
SELF POM-POM, PAGE 28

CAROUSEL HAT, PAGE 46

CARRIE'S CAP, PAGE 105

CITY SNOWFLAKE, PAGE 76

CLARA BOW, PAGE 88

CROCHET BERET, ADULT, PAGE 36

CROCHET BERET, CHILD, PAGE 36

THE CROWN, PAGE 66

DIAMONDS AND LACE, PAGE 78

EASY KNIT HAT, PAGE 33

EASY KNIT HAT,
DEFINING EDGE, PAGE 33

EASY KNIT HAT, RUNNING
STITCH, PAGE 33

EASY-PEASY CROCHET HAT,
SCRUNCH, PAGE 25

EASY-PEASY CROCHET HAT WITH
CROCHET CORKSCREW, PAGE 25

EASY-PEASY CROCHET HAT WITH
EARS, PAGE 24

EASY-PEASY CROCHET HAT WITH
FOLDED TOP, PAGE 24

FLAPPER GRANNY, PAGE 54

HAPPY TRAILS, PAGE 42

I FELT LIKE IT, PAGE 86

THE JESTER, PAGE 68

JUST RIBBING, PAGE 43

THE KISS, PAGE 64

KNIT BERET, ADULT, PAGE 34

KNIT BERET, CHILD, PAGE 34

THE LONG AND SHORT OF IT,
PAGE 102

MANLY SLIP-STITCH HAT, PAGE 74

PAUL BUNYAN, PAGE 99

PORTICO CAP, PAGE 80

PURPLE PILLBOX, PAGE 52

REBEL REBEL, PAGE 94

ROCKY RACCOON, PAGE 61

SUNNY SIDE UP, PAGE 56

SWISS MISS, PAGE 96

URBAN CHULLO, PAGE 71

URBAN TREKKER, PAGE 91

VINTAGE VINES, PAGE 48

INDEX